INSIGHT POCKET GUIDE

CAYMAN ISLANDS

Y0-BDJ-012

APA PUBLICATIONS
Part of the Langenscheidt Publishing Group

4

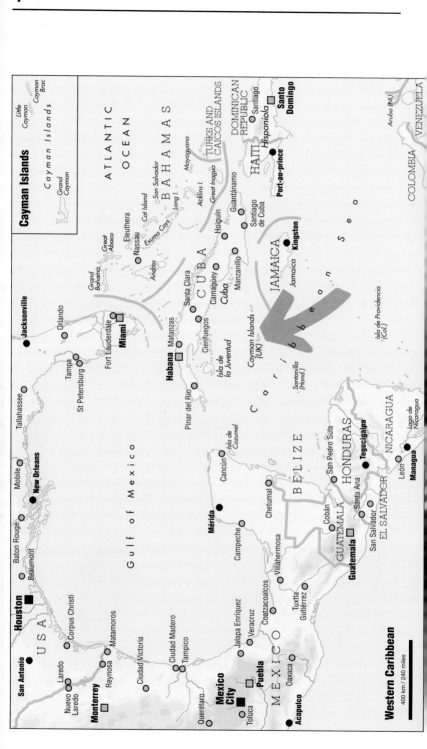

Western Caribbean

400 km / 240 miles

Cayman Islands

Little Cayman
Cayman Brac
Cayman Islands
Grand Cayman

USA

San Antonio
Houston
Corpus Christi
Laredo
Nuevo Laredo
Reynosa
Monterrey
Matamoros
Baton Rouge
Beaumont
New Orleans
Mobile
Tallahassee

Ciudad Victoria
Ciudad Madero
Tampico

Querétaro
Toluca
Mexico City
Puebla
Acapulco
Oaxaca

MEXICO

Jalapa Enriquez
Veracruz
Coatzacoalcos
Villahermosa
Campeche
Mérida
Chetumal
Cancún
Isla de Cozumel

Gulf of Mexico

St Petersburg
Tampa
Orlando
Fort Lauderdale
Miami
Jacksonville

ATLANTIC OCEAN

Tuxtla Gutiérrez
Cobán
GUATEMALA
Guatemala
Santa Ana
San Salvador
EL SALVADOR
San Pedro Sula
Santa Ana
BELIZE
HONDURAS
Tegucigalpa
León
Managua
NICARAGUA
Lago de Nicaragua
Santanilla (Hond.)
Isla de Providencia (Col.)

Caribbean Sea

Pinar del Río
Habana
Matanzas
Cienfuegos
Isla de la Juventud
Santa Clara
CUBA
Cuba
Camagüey
Manzanillo
Holguín
Santiago de Cuba
Guantánamo

Cayman Islands (UK)

JAMAICA
Jamaica
Kingston

Grand Bahama
Great Abaco
Andros
Nassau
Eleuthera
Cat Island
Exuma Cays
San Salvador
Long I.
Acklins I.
BAHAMAS
Great Inagua
Mayaguana
TURKS AND CAICOS ISLANDS

HAITI
Port-au-prince
DOMINICAN REPUBLIC
Santiago
Santo Domingo
Hispaniola

Aruba (Nl)
COLOMBIA
VENEZUELA

Welcome

This guidebook combines the interests and enthusiasm of two of the world's best-known information providers: Insight Guides, who have set the standard for visual travel guides since 1970, and Discovery Channel, the world's premier source of documentary television programming. Its aim is to show readers the best of the Cayman Islands during the course of a series of itineraries devised by Joann Biondi, one of Insight's main correspondents in the Caribbean.

For over 30 years, the Cayman Islands has attracted travelers drawn to the destination's spectacular scuba-diving sites, sophisticated way of life, and casual ambiance. Just 480 miles (772 km) south of Miami, this trio of tropical islands sitting in the crystal-clear Caribbean Sea is a sweet melange of West Indian sassiness, British sensibility, and multicultural cohesiveness. Grand Cayman, the largest of the three, is known throughout the world for its responsible scuba-diving industry, powdery sand beaches, first-class resorts, fine dining, nightlife, and duty-free shopping. The smaller sisters, Cayman Brac and Little Cayman, are environmentally friendly scuba havens with pristine beaches as well, but they are also great escapes from the rigors of the modern world.

The first nine itineraries in this guide concentrate on Grand Cayman, with tours to the bustling capital, historic attractions, the world's only commercial turtle farm, quaint towns, submarine trips, and favorite scuba sites. They are followed by excursions to Cayman Brac and Little Cayman, with four itineraries highlighting things to see and do on those islands, along with round-ups of their most popular scuba sites. The itineraries are supported by sections on history and culture, shopping, eating out, nightlife, a calendar of events, and a detailed practical information that includes a list of hand-picked hotels.

Joann Biondi, a former newspaper reporter, has spent the past 10 years writing about the Caribbean for numerous magazines. A veteran Apa correspondent, she has written seven books for Insight Guides, and teaches Cultural Geography and Travel and Tourism at Miami-Dade Community College. She lives in Miami, which she says is the next best thing to living in the Caribbean.

HISTORY AND CULTURE

ITINERARIES

The first nine tours explore the essential sights and main activities for visitors to Grand Cayman. The following four take in the highlights of neighboring Cayman Brac (tours 10 and 11) and Little Cayman (tours 12 and 13).

Pages 2/3: an interesting underwater encounter
Pages 8/9: dropping anchor at Seven Mile Beach

MORGAN LE FLIBUSTIER

History & Culture

L ike most of the Caribbean, the Cayman Islands have a history inextricably linked to Christopher Columbus, who, on his fourth and final voyage to the New World in 1503, recorded spotting the two small islands now known as Cayman Brac and Little Cayman. Because they were teeming with huge, green sea turtles, he called them *Las Tortugas*.

Unlike most other Caribbean islands, however, there were no indigenous Amerindians living here at the time so no conquest ever took place. In fact, Columbus and his men were so busy repairing their leaky ships and trying desperately to make landfall in Jamaica that they never even set foot in the Cayman Islands. Why there were no indigenous people here remains a mystery. Nearby Jamaica, Cuba, and Haiti all had large Amerindian populations. Historians can only guess that members of the various indigenous groups – Carib, Siboney, Taíno, and Arawak – who must have paddled by in their dugout canoes, considered the flat, arid islands, which had no rivers or lakes, to be too difficult a place to try to forge a life.

During the next 100 years the turtles on the islands became a much-needed food supply for mariners on their way from Jamaica to America. Along with making a sweet-tasting meal, the turtle meat also helped prevent the onslaught of scurvy, and, since they could be kept alive on board ships for months at a time, they also proved to be a convenient staple for the long journeys home to Europe. The name *Las Tortugas*, given by Columbus, did not stick, however, and instead the islands became known as Caymanas. The new name, a Carib Amerindian word meaning crocodile, was just as appropriate, since, along with the turtles, there were thousands of crocodiles inhabiting the islands. After being hunted and eaten by passing sailors for over 300 years, the crocodile population eventually dwindled down to almost zero, but they left the legacy of their name.

Settlers, Slaves, and Pirates

Although they were used as a place to rest and gather food, the Cayman Islands did not receive permanent settlers until the latter half of the 17th century. Oliver Cromwell gained control of Jamaica from the Spanish in 1655, and English dominance of the Cayman Islands soon followed. Then, in 1670, the Treaty of Madrid formally granted English ownership. During the next 100 years the population grew to about 500, including British soldiers, planters, loggers, rope-makers, ship-builders, and a modest number of African slaves. The early settlers, English, Scots and Welsh, did not have an easy life. The harsh,

Left: Sir Henry Morgan, a notorious scoundrel, enjoying life afloat
Right: a 16th-century painting of Columbus

isolated, and inhospitable environment, that was often hit by tropical storms and brutal hurricanes, meant that the harvesting of corn, cotton, yams, plantains, oranges, and limes was a grueling task. It also meant that the settlers were totally dependent on passing ships for other provisions as well as for news from the rest of the world.

Then there was the constant threat of attack from unsavory characters – shipwrecked mariners, army deserters, Spanish conquistadors, and just plain nasty old pirates who considered the entire region a free-for-all, where they

marauded with flagrant greed and grabbed whatever they pleased. Among the more notorious scoundrels who roamed the waters offshore were Sir Henry Morgan, Sir Edward Teach (better known as Blackbeard), and Ann Bonney, one of the few women pirates who ever made it into the history books. Bonney was a member of 'Calico Jack' Rackham's gang when she was arrested and imprisoned in Jamaica. It was from this checkered past of villainous pirates that grand and convoluted tales of buried treasure and hidden skeletons took root throughout the islands.

By 1802 the population had risen to almost 1,000, about half of whom were enslaved Africans. Compared to other nearby islands, where the enslaved population at times constituted over 80 percent, the Cayman Islands never developed into a full-fledged plantation economy fueled by slave labor. Modern historians claim that this is probably the reason why there has never been any serious racial tension or unrest in the Islands.

In 1832, the residents of Grand Cayman gathered at St James Castle and voted to create a legislature of representatives. In 1834 the British Parliament passed an act declaring the emancipation of all enslaved people and the following year all those held in bondage in Cayman were freed. Many of the former slaves either moved to unclaimed land in the interior of the islands, or settled on small parcels of land given to them by their former masters. Others moved to the nearby Bay Islands of Honduras, in the south.

Throughout the 1800s, settlers focused on building a local infrastructure that included schools and churches. It wasn't until the 1830s that small, permanent communities began to spring up on Little Cayman and Cayman Brac. For the most part, local men earned a living as sailors and ship-builders, as fishermen or turtle-harvesters. A few went off to work on the construction of the Panama Canal. Most Caymanian women took care of the homes,

Above: Sir Edward Teach, the English privateer who was more commonly known as Blackbeard the Pirate

raised the children and made thatch-palm products – hats, brooms, and baskets – that they sold locally at markets and exported abroad. The Imperial Act of 1863 formally made the Cayman Islands a dependency of Jamaica, and for the next 20 years the economy flourished, with farming, cattle-rearing, coconut-growing, phosphate-mining, and rope-making.

At the turn of the 20th century the population hit the 5,000 mark, but about 1,500 of these were Caymanian men who frequently left the islands for years at a time to work as merchant marines. In the early 1900s a network of roads was built in Grand Cayman, connecting the various communities on the island. It was also during the early years of the 20th century that the first public buildings were constructed.

In 1953 and 1954 the first airstrips were built on Grand Cayman and Cayman Brac, laying the groundwork for what would become the golden egg of tourism. A few years later tourist hotels were built on Seven Mile Beach and in 1957 dive operator Bob Soto established the first recreational dive shop on Grand Cayman. It was this operation that first introduced visitors to the amazing wonders beneath the calm, aquamarine waters offshore.

Tax-free Status

The Cayman Islands continued to be a dependency of Jamaica until 1962, when the latter chose to become an independent nation and the people of the Cayman Islands voted to hold tight to the Union Jack and become a British Crown Colony instead. Unlike Jamaica, which had a larger population, a vast amount of natural resources, and a rich and fertile landscape capable of producing coffee and sugar, the Cayman Islands saw the prospect of independence as too daunting. Instead, the islands looked toward offshore banking and tourism as their means of economic survival.

In 1966, landmark legislation was passed that paved the way for the development of the banking industry and tax-free status of the islands. Some local historians, however, claim that this concept of tax-free status dates back to 1788, when a convoy of 10 ships carrying merchants from Jamaica to England was wrecked off Grand Cayman and local people rushed to their rescue. King George III of England showed his appreciation for the daring rescue by decreeing the islands a tax-free haven.

In 1967 the national carrier, Cayman Airways, first took to the air; and in 1972 a new constitution was introduced, granting the Cayman Islands autonomy on most domestic issues.

From 1970 to 2001 the islands' population grew from about 10,000 to 36,000. The growth in both the banking and tourism industries has been so phenomenal that there is no longer a need for financial assistance from Great Britain. Because of lax corporate and private tax laws, together with the absence of taxes on personal income or property, the Cayman Islands has become a well-respected hub of international finance during the past three decades or so. With more than 500 international banks in operation, mostly in Grand Cayman, it is now the fifth largest financial center in the world. It is also the world's biggest offshore-island financial center and one of the largest insurance hubs, with about 400 insurance companies maintaining a base in Grand Cayman.

Although no longer in existence, 'secret' tax-free Cayman bank accounts funneled billions of dollars-worth of cold hard cash and slippery electronic funds into the islands during the 1970s and 1980s. At the time, these so-called secret accounts offered a confidentiality clause to account holders as well as numbers rather than names listed on the accounts themselves. Usually, no questions were asked about where the money came from and it's no surprise that accounts like these were a natural magnet for drug smugglers and corrupt politicians from Third World countries. The 1993 feature film, *The Firm*, based on John Grisham's novel, had a plot that included a law firm whose mob clients laundered their cash in the islands. During the 1970s and 1980s thousands of new, modern, concrete houses, apartments, condos, and high-rise hotels were built throughout Grand Cayman, as well as smaller hotels and homes on nearby Cayman Brac.

In 1978 the islands passed the Marine Conservation law, recognizing the importance of the marine environment as a natural resource. Eight years later,

in 1986, the Marine Parks Laws were passed, with the aim of replenishing the marine environment by protecting the coral reefs and marine breeding grounds and regulating all activities that take place in and around the islands' waters. In 1987 the National Trust for the Cayman Islands was established as an independent body to work with the government and local communities in an effort to preserve the local culture, history, flora, fauna, wildlife, and marine environment.

Since then the trust has worked diligently at preserving historic buildings and sites, opening museums, establishing public parks and nature preserves, and protecting public access to beaches and the sea. In 1994 James Manoah Bodden was officially named the first National Hero of the islands. Bodden, a prominent government leader, was primarily responsible for the founding of Cayman Airways and the modernization of Grand Cayman's Owen Roberts International Airport.

Jobs for All

Today, the Cayman Islands enjoys the highest standard of living and the highest per capita income in all the Caribbean (about US$32,000), and there is practically no unemployment. All jobs in the islands must first be offered to a Caymanian and only when there are no local residents available or willing to fill the positions can the work be offered to foreigners. There are so many well-paid jobs that many of the less lucrative service positions are filled by Jamaicans who come to the islands on special work permits. The cost of living, however, is high and consumer goods – cars, houses, clothing, electronics, and foods – are relatively expensive. Also high-priced are the costs of utility services such as telephones, electricity, and Internet service provision.

Above: turtles still flourish at the Cayman Turtle Farm

With over 1.2 million visitors a year, the Cayman Islands is well established as a major, mass-market tourist destination. The first impression that a visitor is likely to have of the place is that of an affluent hamlet. A safe, peaceful, well-managed trio of islands with a sense of British efficiency and old-fashioned manners. Similar in many ways to Bermuda, the Cayman Islands' infrastructure is first-rate and up-to-date and works extremely well. For a group of tiny, isolated islands they are indeed a modern-day success story. There are no visible inner-city slums, no poverty in the countryside, no homeless people, no beggars, and no street hustlers harassing tourists, as can be seen elsewhere in the region. Nor are there any gambling casinos, a characteristic linked to the fact that the conservative-minded Christian churches on the islands hold a great deal of sway.

Birds and Beasts

Away from the concrete ribbon of modern hotels and high-rise condos that line Grand Cayman's Seven Mile Beach, there are still many pristine places to be found, where local people are eager to talk to visitors and the pace of life is molasses slow. Old, tropical-style cottages with breezy verandahs and bold Caribbean colors dot many nooks and crannies away from the main tourist areas. And even a few traditional wattle and daub houses remain. Although no longer built, these old homes were constructed with iron-wood posts, woven cabbage-wood walls, and a thick mortar called daub that was used to coat the entire structure. Extremely labor-intensive to construct, the houses were sturdy enough to withstand hurricanes.

Turtles have always lived on the islands. As we know, Columbus mentioned them in his log and named the islands after them, and turtle farming remains an important industry. Still abundant, due to a successful breeding program at the Cayman Turtle Farm, the large, green sea turtle is a national symbol and its image can be found on flags, currency, souvenirs, the official government seal and even on the jets in the Cayman Airways fleet.

What is most striking about the Cayman Islands, and the rea-

Above: the little Cayman iguana is probably the most striking of the indigenous creatures. **Right:** a vividly-colored parrot, one of numerous exotic birds

son why most people come here, is how Mother Nature struts her stuff. First of all there's the sea and the kaleidoscope of colors that lie beneath it – stunning coral reefs, winding ravines, pinnacles, caves, sponges, sea fans, hermit crabs, starfish, sharks, and an array of tropical fish that cause the jaws of even the best-traveled divers to drop in awe. Next comes the bright yellow sun that shines non-stop throughout the year. And then there is the tropical landscape and the unusual creatures that inhabit it.

The islands are blessed with a natural bounty of flora and fauna. There are mangrove swamps, red birch, tropical ferns, bamboo, pine, coconut groves, bananas, figs, royal poinciana trees, wild sorrel, hibiscus, frangipani, heliconia, bird of paradise, anthuriums, morning glory vines, cactus, orchids, and bromeliads. Among the creatures to look out for are the Grand Cayman and Cayman Brac parrots, endemic birds with iridescent green feathers and reddish-orange necks that live in the interior of the islands and feed on berries from the interestingly named gumbo limbo tree.

About 20,000 red-footed boobies live primarily on Little Cayman and snowy egrets, frigates, humming birds, doves, herons, ospreys, swallows, terns, warblers, woodpeckers, black-headed stilts, quits, vireos, plovers, ducks, owls, and thrushes can all be found just about everywhere. There are also more than 50 species of butterfly and during the summer months their white, fluttering bodies fill the air.

Magnificent Iguanas

A small, rabbit-like animal called an agouti can often be spotted scurrying around densely wooded areas; and frogs, bats, centipedes, caterpillars, nocturnal geckos, mongooses, and non-poisonous snakes are also common. But the most exotic and strikingly handsome creature is, without a doubt, the iguana. Grand Cayman is home to the endangered and endemic Blue Iguana and locals claim that there are only about 150 of them living in the wild along the eastern end of the island. On Little Cayman there are about 2,000

Little Cayman Rock Iguanas that can grow up to 6 ft (2 m) long. On this tiny island, they are often seen strolling around as if they own the joint. Usually slow-moving and lazy, they can be found foraging through the mangroves in search of ripe papayas that have fallen from the surrounding trees.

When visitors come upon them, as they often do, the iguanas just ignore the interruption and go about their business. Unless, of course, the intruders have come prepared with a bag of fresh grapes or slices of orange that they intend to share. Then, the iguanas amble forward and graciously accept the treat.

Above: James Manoah Bodden, the islands' first official National Hero

HISTORY HIGHLIGHTS

1503 Christopher Columbus sights the islands and names them *Las Tortugas* (meaning turtles, in Spanish). Over the next 100 years, the name Cayman comes into common usage.

1586 A fleet of 23 ships, under the direction of privateer, Sir Frances Drake, stops for two days in Grand Cayman. The islands are uninhabited, but Drake makes note of the many turtles, crocodiles, alligators, and iguanas he sees.

1670 Under the terms of the Treaty of Madrid, Spain recognizes England's sovereignty over Jamaica and the Cayman Islands.

1773 The population reaches 400, and the Royal Navy makes its first map of Grand Cayman.

1790 Fort George is constructed to ward off attacks by the French and Spanish.

1794 The 'Wreck of the Ten Sails' take place off the coast of Grand Cayman.

1831 A decision is made to form a new assembly, and the islands' first legislation is passed. The population reaches 2,000.

1830s First missionaries from the Anglican Church arrive. A church is built in George Town, and the first schools are established.

1835 Governor Sligo of Jamaica lands in Cayman to declare all enslaved people free, in accordance with the Emancipation Act of 1833.

1863 An Act of the Imperial Parliament in London declares the Cayman Islands a dependency of Jamaica.

1898 Frederick Sanguinetti, an official of the Jamaican Government, is appointed the first Commissioner of the Cayman Islands.

1911 The population reaches 5,500.

1920 Education Act passes, providing for schools in all districts.

1937 The first cruise ship, the *Atlantis*, sails into port and tourism begins to take hold.

1942–45 A US Naval Base and a Coast Guard Base are founded on Grand Cayman.

1953 A new airport is opened in Grand Cayman, replacing the old seaplane base.

1950s Dozens of new hotels open throughout the island

1957 Bob Soto establishes the first recreational diving operation in the Caribbean on Grand Cayman.

1959 Caymanian women are granted the right to vote; the Cayman Islands cease to be a dependency of Jamaica.

1962 Following Jamaica's independence from Great Britain, the Cayman Islands choose to remain a Crown Colony.

1966 Landmark banking legislation is introduced, paving the way for the tax-free status of the islands.

1967 Cayman Airways, the national carrier, takes to the air.

1972 The new Caymanian Constitution is introduced.

1978 Cayman Islands passes the Marine Conservation Law to protect offshore waters.

1986 The Marine Parks Law goes into effect, further insuring protection of marine life in the islands.

1987 The National Trust is created to preserve the natural, historic, and maritime heritage of the islands.

1994 James Manoah Bodden, government leader and co-founder of Cayman Airways, is designated the country's first National Hero.

2000 Jean-Michel Cousteau is named official spokesperson for diving in the Cayman Islands.

2001 The population of the Cayman Islands reaches 36,000.

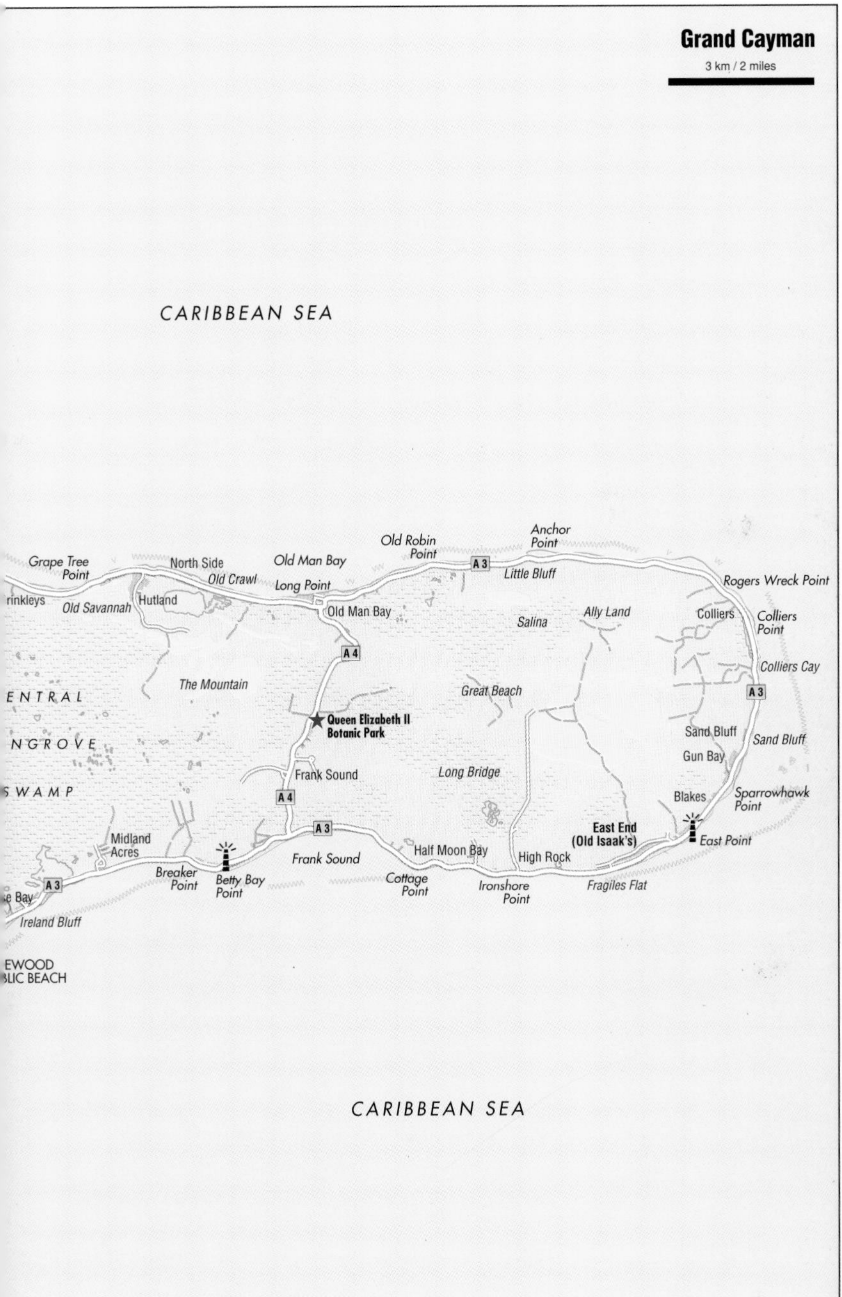

Grand Cayman

3 km / 2 miles

CARIBBEAN SEA

Grape Tree Point

North Side

Old Man Bay

Old Robin Point

Anchor Point

A 3

Little Bluff

Rogers Wreck Point

rinkleys

Old Savannah

Hutland

Old Crawl

Long Point

Old Man Bay

Salina

Ally Land

Colliers

Colliers Point

A 4

Great Beach

Colliers Cay

A 3

The Mountain

ENTRAL

★ Queen Elizabeth II Botanic Park

Sand Bluff

Sand Bluff

NGROVE

Frank Sound

Long Bridge

Gun Bay

SWAMP

A 4

Blakes

Sparrowhawk Point

Midland Acres

A 3

Frank Sound

Half Moon Bay

East End (Old Isaak's)

East Point

Breaker Point

Betty Bay Point

Cottage Point

High Rock

e Bay

A 3

Ironshore Point

Fragiles Flat

Ireland Bluff

EWOOD
BLIC BEACH

CARIBBEAN SEA

Orientation

With three separate and uniquely different islands to choose from, a tour of the Cayman Islands nearly always means several days spent in Grand Cayman, and then an excursion of another two or three days to either Cayman Brac or Little Cayman.

Lying south of Miami and Cuba, and northwest of Jamaica, the islands have a history inextricably linked to Britain. Today there is still a hint of Britishness about these tropical isles that steadfastly remain a British territory.

Aside from the fantastic dive sites that can be found around all three of the islands, Grand Cayman is where you will find a plethora of first-class hotels and resorts, fine restaurants, sizzling nightlife, duty-free shopping centers, and historic attractions. It is also the island that attracts the majority of visitors, including thousands of cruise ship passengers who debark in the capital, George Town, each day.

The largest of the three islands, Grand Cayman is 28 miles (45 km) long and 7 miles (11 km) wide, with a population of about 34,000. Excellent roads throughout the island make touring the sites easy and convenient with either a rental car or hired taxi *(see Practical Information, pages 84–85)*. Explore George Town's fort and museums, bask on stunning Seven Mile Beach, or enjoy nature's bountiful mangrove in the interior, and the breath-taking Blow Holes in the East End.

If you really want to spend your time on deserted beaches and intentionally disconnect from the hustle and bustle of the modern world, Cayman Brac or Little Cayman (89 miles/143 km and 74 miles/120 km northeast of Grand Cayman respectively and accessed by plane from George Town) are the islands to visit for a peaceful interlude and a back-to-nature experience. Your most likely companions on these islands will be iguanas, exotic birds, an array of marine life, and very few humans.

Planning your Visit

For an ideal Cayman Islands vacation it is suggested that you pick and choose from the nine tours listed in the Grand Cayman section and find the particular choices that suit your special interests – sites of historic significance, botanical gardens and nature trails, submarine trips, water-sports such as scuba diving and snorkeling, or visiting an interesting little town called Hell. Then, decide on which of the two 'sister' islands – Cayman Brac or Little Cayman – you would like to see and plan an additional excursion around it.

Left: vividly-colored coral
Right: the pace of life is slow on the islands

Grand Cayman

1. A GEORGE TOWN WALKABOUT   *(see map below)*

A leisurely walk through downtown George Town with visits to Fort George, the Elmslie United Memorial Church, the Cayman Islands National Museum, and the historic Pantonville houses. The walk can be completed in two to three hours, and is best done early in the morning before the afternoon traffic jams cause gridlock.

Comfortable shoes and a sun hat are suggested. You can also check in advance with the Tourist Board to find out the cruise-ship schedule and plan your tour to avoid the rush.

Small, compact, and easy to explore on foot, the capital city of George Town makes for a very pleasant morning walk. Although it is dense with banks and insurance companies, it is also full of important historic sites and attractive old buildings with architectural styles that include Victorian, Georgian, Colonial, and West Indian. It also has a numerous modern stores, cafés, and restaurants.

With a not-so-pleasant original name of Hogsties (wild boar were penned here to provide food for the crews of passing ships in the 17th century), the new name of George Town came about in the late 1700s and was created to honor Britain's King George III. For the record, there aren't any hogs wandering around the town. Free, historic walking tour maps published by the National Trust for the Cayman Islands are available from the Tourist Board or the Cayman Islands National Museum, and provide helpful information for a self-guiding tour.

Most of the action in downtown George Town takes place near the harbor, and a logical place to begin a walking tour is at **Fort George** on Harbour Drive near Fort Street. Although it's right on the water-front, the fort is easy to miss since there isn't very much of it left. Built in 1790 as a defense against Spanish invaders from nearby Cuba, the original fort was oval in shape and made out of solid coral rock with walls 5 ft (1.5 m) thick. It wasn't as large as most other forts in the Caribbean, but it was strate-gically located to ward off attacks. During World War II it was used

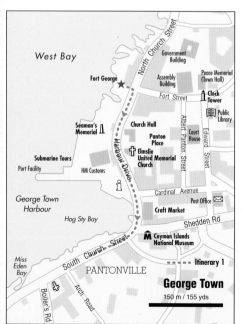

by the Cayman Islands Home Guard (the local militia) as a guard tower to watch for the German submarines that often patrolled the Caribbean. To make way for new construction in the area, a real estate developer demolished the fort in 1972, much to the chagrin of local historians who staged a protest on the waterfront. In 1987 the remains were deeded to the National Trust, which then conducted an archaeological dig that retrieved dozens of priceless artifacts that are now displayed in the Cayman Islands National

Museum. Today, all that remains are three small portions of the wall, two long cannons, an old look-out hut made of native wood, and the stunning panoramic view. Near the fort is the **Seaman's Memorial**, which pays tribute to the islands' long seafaring history, and lists the names of 153 Caymanians who lost their lives at sea.

Cayman's Cathedral

Continuing south on Harbour Drive, you will come to two cruise-ship terminals, the **North Terminal** and the **South Terminal**. Almost identical, they handle several hundred thousand passengers each year who debark at this spot for tours of the island. They both have public toilets that are always kept neat and clean. Across the street from the terminals on Harbour Drive is the **Elmslie United Memorial Church** (Mon–Fri 9am–5pm, with services on Sunday at 9.30am and 11am; tel: 949 7923). Named for one of the first Presbyterian ministers in Grand Cayman, who served on the island from 1846 to 1863, and built in 1920 by noted ship-builder Captain Rayal Bodden, the church is an impressive structure with a timber roof shaped like an upturned schooner hull. Constructed on the site of the original church that

dated from 1835, it is often called 'Cayman's very own cathedral.' During the 1860s, the Elmslie Church group established six other churches on the island and had a congregation of over 400 people.

This church was the first building in the Cayman Islands constructed out of concrete blocks, and Captain Bodden visited Jamaica beforehand to learn how to make the concrete molds. Inside, the sleek mahogany

Top: the simple exterior of the Elmslie Church
Above: the *George Town Galleon* sets sail

pews were crafted by another local ship-builder, and the ceiling was made from wood salvaged from old sailing ships. The bold-colored stained-glass windows were donated by Dr Roy McTaggert, a local man often credited with persuading Caymanians to retain British colony status. Recently restored to its original condition, it also contains several memorial plaques and old, stone grave markers shaped like small houses. Set amid the bright and noisy commercial district of downtown George Town, it offers a cool and contemplative respite from the relentless hot sun.

The National Museum

Farther along on Harbour Drive, past several little stores, you will spot a sprawling island-style white building with a bright red roof and a flagpole out front. This is the **Cayman Islands National Museum** (open Mon–Fri 9am–5pm, Sat 10am–2pm; admission fee; tel: 949 8368), a treasure chest that serves as the Cayman Islands collective memory and link to the past. One of the finest museums in the Caribbean, it first opened in 1990, and is now one of the more popular attractions in the city. The museum got its start in the 1950s when a local man named Ira Thompson started collecting 'odds and ends' of Caymanian history. A professional driver by trade, Thompson's collection grew so large that he opened the Cayman Museum in a small building on South Church Street. For his dedication to island history, Thompson was awarded a Certificate of Honor by Elizabeth II of Britain, and eventually he donated all his artifacts to the government, which later created this new museum.

Housed in the city's Old Courthouse, that dates back to the 1830s, it is the second oldest surviving building in Grand Cayman and a classic example of a Caymanian 'upstairs house.' The first floor is constructed of wattle and daub, and the second floor – complete with verandah – is made of framed timber.

Top: the Cayman Islands National Museum, one of the finest in the Caribbean. **Right:** a little boy with a serious view on life

Green wooden hurricane shutters adorn all the windows. It once had a large lantern on top that helped sailors of the day to navigate the port. Through the years, the building has played many roles in the city, including parsonage, court house, post office, library, and jail. The dozen steps that lead to the top floor, which once housed the court room, brought the local expression 'walking the twelve steps' into being and means that you are about to pay the price for your bad deeds.

Inside is a stunning array of over 2,000 artifacts that draw on the history of the islands. Near the entrance-way is an air-conditioned theater that runs a continuous 10-minute audiovisual display on Caymanian culture and history. Departing the theater, you walk through a display that depicts each stage of the traditional building technique known as wattle and daub. Around the corner you come to the **Natural History Exhibit** with a three-dimensional depiction of the undersea mountains and canyons offshore, including an excellent diagram explaining the Cayman Trench. It also has educational displays of dry woodlands, beach sand, swamps, shells, caymanite, and indigenous plants and trees. Nearby is a submarine's porthole that contains a fish tank filled with moray eels and tropical fish. The museum's **Cultural History Gallery** hosts rotating exhibits that focus on the people of the Cayman Islands. Other rooms contain a collection of furniture made by Wilbanks Miller, a highly regarded ship's carpenter who was born in 1881, as well as tools, cooking utensils, sisal switches used to swat mosquitos, and thick leather sandals, commonly called 'wompers,' that were worn by early settlers.

Historic Pantonville

Back on the street, just two blocks south of the museum down an unmarked dirt lane, is a collection of historic buildings known as **Pantonville**. These attractive, two-story houses with their ornate gingerbread trim and gabled roofs were built by the local Panton family, and several of their ancestors are buried here. One of the larger houses was owned by Bernie Panton who used wood salvaged from a ship named *Balboa* that sank in the George Town harbor in 1932, to add on the second-floor verandah. The single-story structure in the center is also a Panton house, and was built more than 100 years ago by Albert Panton. During its heyday, Albert Panton's house was the talk of the town because of its rare, wood-burning iron stove. Today, most of the houses are used as offices by local business people. Also in this little Pantonville district is **Merrendale**, the 1870 home of the Merrens, a well-known Caymanian merchant family.

Shopping and Exploring

On the streets surrounding Pantonville there are dozens of art galleries, restaurants, and outdoor cafés. And, of course, the world-famous duty-free shopping centers that attract thousands of cruise-ship passengers each day

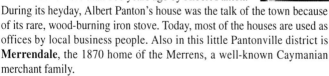

Right: the British Outpost is a good place to shop for excellent duty-free jewelry

with their dazzling displays of discount gold watches, designer clothing, perfumes, cosmetics, luggage, crystal, electronics, liquor, leather goods, diamond and emerald jewelry, and hand-rolled premium cigars.

Other points of interest in the downtown area include the **Cayman Islands National Archives** (Mon–Fri 9am–5pm; free; tel: 949 9809), off Crewe Road near Thomas Russell Way, which are full of historic materials, such as births and deaths records from the 19th century. On Cardinal Avenue is the **Farmers' Market**, a shopping center that supplies local people with fresh fruits, vegetables, meat, fish, and home-made cakes. Close by is the **Craft Market**, a favorite stop for tourists shopping for island-made souvenirs.

At the intersection of Fort and Edward Street is the **Clock Tower**. Built in 1937 in honor of King George V, the tower is just one of many monuments in the city that characterize the Caymanian allegiance to Great Britain. Opposite the Clock Tower is the **Peace Memorial**, built in 1919, which served as the Town Hall for many years and was the center of life in the city, hosting everything from playful community dances to important political meetings. It was in this building that the Cayman Islands officially voted to forgo independence in 1962. It is most noted, however, for the fact that it was dedicated in the name of peace rather than war.

Also on Edward Street is the **Public Library**, erected in 1939 and well stocked with books on Cayman Islands history and culture. Built by Captain Bodden, who was also responsible for the Elmslie Church on Harbour Drive, the library has a timbered ceiling decorated with ornate shields from many of the finest universities in Great Britain. Directly behind the library is an area of the city that was used by the US Navy during World War II. Here, while conducting social functions and filming news reports, several US officers met and fell in love with Caymanian women who eventually became known as island war brides.

Above: there's plenty of room to play on Seven Mile Beach

2. SEVEN MILE BEACH/WEST BAY/HELL *(see map, p28)*

Venture up the glorious coast of Seven Mile Beach, mail the requisite postcards from Hell, and visit the world-renowned Cayman Turtle Farm.

Grand Cayman's **Seven Mile Beach** prides itself on being a self-contained vacation paradise where visitors can find everything they need – and it's perfectly true. This highly developed stretch of white, sandy beach is jam-packed with hotels, resorts, condominiums, restaurants, bars, stores, water-sports and dive operators, and is the nucleus of the island's tourism industry. But it is also congested, and can at times feel more like Miami Beach than a Caribbean island resort.

Sandwiched between the North Sound and the sea, Seven Mile Beach begins at the northern outskirts of George Town and is technically only about 6 miles (10 km) long. Most of the commercial development is along the southern half, and after that it mellows out into a quiet residential neighborhood, dotted with a few small hotels. The beach itself is absolutely stunning, with clear, calm water that is ideal for swimming.

To the north of Seven Mile Beach the road enters **West Bay**, the second largest district in Grand Cayman, with a population of about 8,000. Here, the name of the main thoroughfare changes to North West Point Road and the atmosphere becomes more residential. First settled in the 1740s, West Bay was once a community of turtle hunters and mariners who braved the dreaded mosquito-carried malaria that once plagued the area.

A century or so later, substantial phosphate deposits led to the development of a mining industry, and by the 1780s this was the main source of income in the area. However, in the early 1900s better-quality deposits were discovered in Florida and the industry here went bust.

Inland from the coast, West Bay has a large local community, and is graced with cow pastures, schools, football (soccer) fields, and churches. One church in particular, the **West Bay United Church** (usually open during daylight hours; services Sunday 9am and 7pm) is especially interesting. The church was designed to resemble a classic Cayman-ian sailing ship and has a pulpit made of local mahogany, as well as stunning stained-glass windows depicting Christ calling fishermen home.

Local Insights

Continuing north, the road comes to one of the few stop-lights in the area and a tiny building in a little shopping center appears. This is **Powell's Heritage Museum** (Mon–Thur 10am–5pm; admission fee; tel: 949 3477). The passion of a native Caymanian, Tony Powell, this hot and dusty, privately-owned museum is housed in an old general store and is filled with an illuminating collection of island artifacts. Farming tools, books, letters, maps, prayer books, school report cards, photographs, fishing equipment,

Above: the Devil's Hangout is on every visitor's itinerary

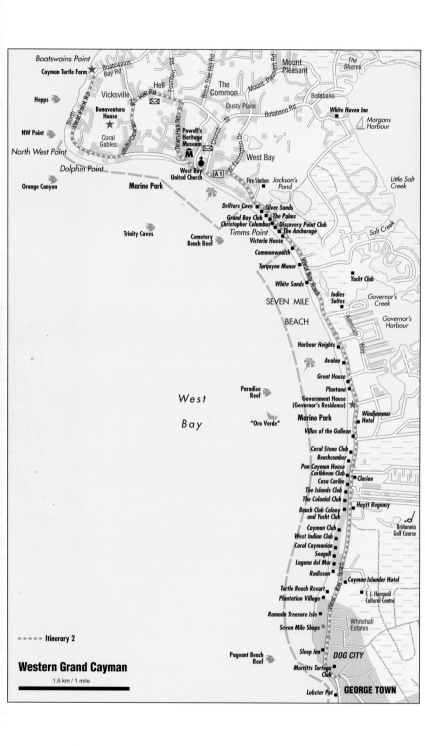

sewing machines, and old documents are all on display, and wandering around the museum feels like making a visit to grandma's house.

To Hell and Back

Just beyond the stop-light at the museum, the road forks and a rusty white sign with an arrow pointing to **Hell** appears. This area, a maze of tiny back roads that traverse small hills, is very easy to get lost in, and many people joke that they never thought they'd have a hard time going to Hell. After driving about a half a mile (1 km) along this road (which has no name), you will spot another sign that says Hell Road and in no time you will see the fleet of air-conditioned tour buses that cart about 500 cruise-ship passengers here every day. Although it is easily classified as a tourist trap, Hell is a cheerful place where most visitors have a great time.

Full of kitsch and kick, the so-called town consists of a gas station, post office, and about six gift shops. One of those shops, the **Devil's Hangout** (daily 7am–5pm; tel: 949 1087), is on everyone's itinerary. As visitors walk in the door, owner Ivan Farrington greets them with his standard repertoire: 'Welcome to the coolest place in Hell.' 'How the hell are you?' 'Where the hell are you from?' 'What the hell do you want?'

Usually dressed in a frilly tuxedo shirt, black bow tie, red cape, and red horns, Farrington is a native-born Caymanian who has lived on Hell Road ever since he was a child. A local legend who has become a media darling with travel magazines and CNN's travel channel, he's a natural-born performer, whose business card says: 'For a date with the Devil call Ivan Farrington.'

As in the other gift shops, the shelves here are stocked with Hot-as-Hell pepper sauce, diplomas from the University of Hell, and cups, plates and spoons emblazoned with fiery Hell logos. And, of course, souvenir T-shirts that say: 'Been to Hell and Back,' and 'Never Tell Your Mother to go to Hell Because She'll Buy You One of these Stupid Shirts and Make You Wear it to School.'

Top: an observation deck overlooks the stark, black rocks of Hell
Right: even in Hell, you mustn't drop litter

Bleak, Black Rocks

How Hell got its name is part of local lore on the island. In the early 1930s, Commissioner Cardinal from Britain was visiting the West Bay District and decided to do some bird hunting. Rifle in hand, he aimed for one lone heron sitting amid a vast field of stark, grayish, blackish rocks, and said, 'This place looks like Hell.' The name stuck. Just for the record, the commissioner missed his shot.

The bleak and desolate rocks that caught the commissioner's eye do, in fact, look like the charred remains of an inferno, and are the main attraction of a visit to Hell. A winding wooden walkway behind the gift shops leads visitors to an observation deck that overlooks acres and acres of the natural mass of pinnacles and ridges. A black statue of the devil stands guard, perhaps to reinforce the several signs sternly warning visitors that 'The Removal of Hell Rocks is Prohibited.'

According to geologists, the brittle, pockmarked rocks are over one million years old, and are the result of a chemical reaction involving limestone, calcium, and magnesium. They were then transformed even more by thousands of years of interaction with brackish water and pockets of algae.

More commonly known as dolomite, in the Cayman Islands this porous, sedimentary rock is called iron-shore. The official scientific name is phytokarst. The prefix – phyto – means plant, and the suffix – karst – means eroded landform. At the base of the rocks are shallow pools of brackish water full of schools of minnows rushing around.

One of Mother Nature's more bizarre creations, this bleak landscape evokes a hauntingly eerie, Dante-esque mood. The rocks' pinnacles are so sharp they're almost impossible to walk on. Island children are told ghost stories about evil spirits that inhabit the rocks, and teenage couples (prepared to brave the demons) often come here late at night in search of privacy.

Above: the Cayman Turtle Farm plays a serious environmental role

grand cayman

Every now and then, especially at Christmas, local people float a coat of oil on the water and set the rocks on fire.

There's one thing that most people who come here just can't resist – mailing a postcard from Hell. The **Hell Post Office** (Mon–Fri 8.30am–5pm, Sat 8.30am–noon) is a modern little facility known for its clever postmark, and well equipped to handle the hordes of tourists who come in to buy stamps and drop off their cards before they leave.

Turtle Time

After leaving Hell and getting back to North Bay Road, continue northward and in less than a mile (1.5 km) you will find the **Cayman Turtle Farm** (daily 8.30am–5pm; admission fee; tel: 949 3894). One of the most-visited places in the Cayman Islands, and the only one of its kind in the world, the Turtle Farm is much more than a tourist attraction. Rooted deep in the Cayman culture, the turtle has always represented a way of life and livelihood that today has almost disappeared. Now an endangered species, the green sea turtles were on their way to extinction in the islands until the Turtle Farm came to the rescue.

Founded in 1968 to breed and raise turtles commercially, the farm has successfully implemented a breed-and-release program that has returned over 30,000 tagged turtles to the wild. Many of them return to Cayman Island beaches to nest their eggs, and they are often spotted by divers offshore. Others have been seen as far away as Venezuela, Nicaragua, Panama, and Mexico.

Each year the farm produces on average over 10,000 hatchlings. The mating season occurs between April and July, with eggs being laid a few months later. Females usually lay five to seven clutches, each containing approximately 100 eggs. The eggs at the farm are collected at the time of laying and transferred to incubators, where the temperature is maintained at 82° F (26.6° C). The temperature determines the sex of the turtle, and this temperature control ensures an equal number of males and females hatched. If the temperature drops just a few degrees, the result is all male turtles. If it's any warmer, it means all females.

Each egg takes 60 days to hatch, and then the fragile babies are transferred to sand boxes for a few days before being placed in water again. Weighing only a few ounces, the babies are fed a special diet that enables them to grow to about 8–10 ins (20–25 cm) long and weigh 6 lbs (2.7 kg) in one year.

The farm is a land-based operation and the turtles are raised in enormous tanks filled with seawater that is pumped in fresh every day. As visitors walk into the compound, they are awestruck by the sight of over 16,000 turtles gracefully swimming around with their heads bobbing and flippers flapping.

A concrete walkway takes visitors past the tanks that each contain turtles of the same

Right: feeding time for the turtles

size. Ranging from the cute little babies to fully mature ones weighing in at 600 lbs (272 kg), the creatures appear strong and healthy and not at all bothered by the fact that they are held in captivity. The breeding herd of 300, some of them more than 50 years old, is kept in large deep pool at the center of the farm. There is also a sandy, man-made beach where females are placed to lay their eggs.

Exact feeding times vary, but as a rough guide the turtles are fed early in the morning and again late in the afternoon, and the commotion in the water when this takes place is thrilling, so these are obviously the best times to visit. While visitors are asked not to touch or feed them, many of the turtles are quite friendly and swim right up to people leaning over the tanks.

In addition to the turtles released into the wild, quite a large number of them wind up as delicacies on the menus of island restaurants. Turtle meat has for centuries been a dietary staple of the Caymanian community, and environmentalists believe that satisfying the local demand for turtle meat in this way eliminates the need to hunt the creatures in the wild, and is in the long run good for the turtle population.

Along with the breeding program, the farm is a major research center and scientists from universities throughout the world come here to conduct studies on the social behavior, aging, stress, and population dynamics of the species. It also does valuable conservation work by educating the tens of thousands of visitors who come here each year. Although the turtles are, of course, the main event, there are also several other indigenous animals on display, such as Cayman green parrots, rock iguanas, crocodiles, and agouti (an indigenous species rather like a small rabbit).

3. STINGRAY CITY *(see map, p18)*

A trek to Stingray City, considered one of the world's top dive sites, to snorkel and feed the stingrays. While it's a delightful thing to do, snorkeling in Stingray City can be an intense experience for first-timers.

Wearing a T-shirt and sunblock lotion while in the water is advised. Several operators offer tours to Stingray City that include snorkeling gear, drinks and snacks, as well as the boat ride. Prices range from US$25–50 per person. Depending on how many stops the boats make, the tours last from four to six hours.

Top of the list of things to do in Grand Cayman must be an excursion to Stingray City. To miss it would be a bit like visiting Rome and not taking in the Coliseum. It's something you've just got to do – and if you don't, you'll regret it.

Right: stingrays should only be touched with bare hands, to protect their skin

grand cayman

Located in the North Sound, between West Bay and Rum Point, Stingray City is often called the best 12-ft (3.5-meter) dive in the world. It consists of two distinct spots – **Stingray City** itself, and the **Sandbar** – two shallow, sheltered areas in calm, clear waters, with coral heads, a barrier reef, and literally hundreds of the curious stingrays.

Both Stingray City and the Sandbar have been featured in *National Geographic* magazine as among the most spectacular dive locations in the world. At Stingray City,

snorkelers swim round a sandbar while the rays play in the water around them. At the Sandbar, the water is so shallow that you can actually stand up and wade through it while dozens of rays swim around your feet, so it is ideal for children and non-swimmers.

The reason there are so many stingrays in the vicinity is that, many years ago, local fishermen used to come here to clean their catch before bringing it ashore, and they would dump the unwanted remains in the water. After a while, the stingrays just naturally began congregating in the area, knowing that they could expect an easy meal.

For Novices and Experts Alike

Although boat-loads of visitors now come here each day to share this unusual experience, it remains a prominent dive site and even 'serious' divers still like to use it. While some visitors come equipped with full scuba gear, most find that just a mask and snorkel is all they need. In fact, people who don't even know how to swim are able to take in the Stingray City experience. After decades as a tourist attraction, the rays have grown accustomed to all the action and usually swoop in and swarm around the boats as soon as they arrive. Ranging in size from 2 ft to 5 ft (60 cm to 1.5 m) wide, they are not at all shy about accepting a free meal and will either bump into you or rub up against your body if they sense you have food and are holding out on them. They will also glide right by you flapping their 'wings' as a signal, in case you had failed to notice them. Every now and then some nosy fish (usually groupers or snappers) will come by, trying to get a piece of the action. The food – which is usually tidbits of raw squid – is brought to the site by the dive masters and then doled out by hand.

Above: stingrays swoop and swarm around boats and curious visitors

Southern stingrays – their proper name is *Dasyatis Americana* – don't bite, but they do have sharp pointers on their tails that can sting a person's skin quite seriously, hence their name. As they pass by, you can reach out and touch their velvety undersides and they won't be perturbed. But, as the dive masters will warn you, you should touch them only with your bare hands, because diving gloves can remove the protective mucous that coats their skin.

It is a great experience to feed the creatures yourself but be prepared for the feeding frenzy that churns the water when you do so. And remember to hold the palm of your hand out flat with the food on it, as if you were feeding a horse, so that the rays don't nip your skin by mistake.

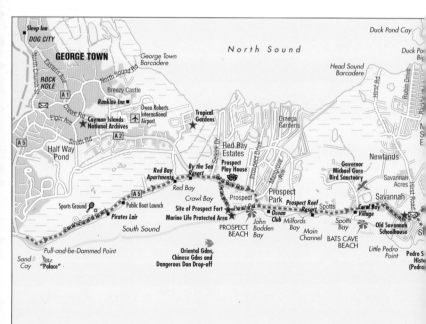

Above: the Pedro St James Historic Site, a magnificently restored building

4. THE SOUTHEAST COAST *(see map below)*

A glimpse of the historic side of Grand Cayman with a ride along the Southeast Coast, taking in Prospect, Savanna, Pedro St James Historic Site, and Bodden Town.

Just a few miles east of George Town, Grand Cayman has several interesting spots where the history of the islands comes vividly to life. Heading east from the capital along South Sound Road, past the luxury homes and sprawling estates that line the waterfront here, the highway turns into Red Bay Road and continues through **Prospect**. Although all that is left to mark its historic significance is a small, hard-to-find monument, Prospect was once the site of a massive, 18th-century fort that was built to defend the island from pirates. In 1846, a terrible hurricane wiped out the fort and most of the houses and buildings in the surrounding area.

Nearby is the **Watler Cemetery**, a family burial ground that contains the remains of the Watler family, who were among the earliest settlers on the island, back in the early 1700s. Their descendants donated this land to the National Trust for the Cayman Islands in 1991, to be turned into an historic monument. Open to the public, the cemetery is surrounded by an old stone wall and has dozens of graves with well-maintained tombstones decorated with coral rocks and seashells.

A few miles past the cemetery is the **Governor Michael Gore Bird Sanctuary**, a lush 3.5-acre (1.5-ha) spread of land that contains thousands of birds indigenous to the Cayman Islands. Just past the sanctuary is the town of **Savannah**. The first building of significance here is the **Old**

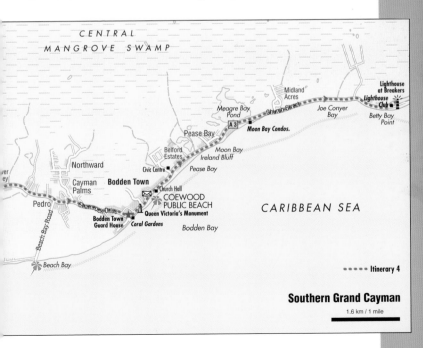

Southern Grand Cayman

1.6 km / 1 mile

Savannah Schoolhouse, built in 1940 and recently restored by the National Trust. Surrounded by a garden of pink, purple, and white periwinkle flowers, the one-room schoolhouse closed for classes in 1981 when a more modern school was built nearby, but it remains as a reminder of days gone by.

Pedro St James

The major attraction of Savannah, and the most important historic site on the entire island, is **Pedro St James Historic Site** (daily 9am–5pm; admission fee; tel: 947 3329). Also

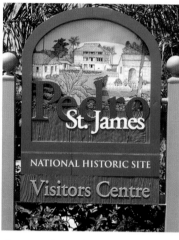

known as Pedro Castle, this magnificently-restored great house is considered by local people to be the birthplace of democracy in the Cayman Islands. Signs on the highway clearly mark the turn-off point that leads down a bumpy street to the site entrance. Once inside the property, guests pass through the impressive Visitors' Centre and gift shop with a modern, air-conditioned restaurant right next door. Close to the Visitors' Centre is a comfortable theater that runs a continuous, state-of-the-art, 24-minute multimedia presentation depicting the role Pedro St James played in Caymanian history.

Perched on a limestone cliff with panoramic views of Old Jones Bay and surrounded by formal English gardens, the great house at St James was originally built by William Eden from Wiltshire in England in 1780 and is the oldest stone structure still standing in Grand Cayman. Sturdy and well built, it has survived the numerous hurricanes that have wiped out most other historic structures on the island. Lush green lawns dotted with palms and flowering plants flow down from the house, and there's a walk around the peaceful 7-acre (2.8-ha) property that offers a realistic view of what colonial life was like hundreds of years ago.

Constructed by slave labor, the three-story main house is made of native stone with outer walls 3 ft (1 m) thick, and dark-green wooden louvers on every window for protection from the weather. It is a classic manor-type house with a gabled roof and outside staircase. On the first floor there is a large kitchen adjoined by two smaller rooms, one of which was sometimes used as a jail cell to hold criminals before they were shipped off to Jamaica for trial.

The second floor houses the formal dining room surrounded by wrap-around verandahs, and the bedrooms and sitting room are on the third floor. Restored to their original condition, all the rooms are furnished with period antiques and artifacts, including mahogany tables, rocking chairs, four-poster beds, earthenware storage jars, silverware, wrought-iron candelabras, cooking utensils, old photographs, linens, and lace curtains.

Top: a welcoming sign outside the Pedro St James Historic Site
Above: small children pose for a picture

It was at Pedro St James in 1831 that local citizens gathered to plot their future and formalize plans to hold elections on the island. Prior to this date most decisions concerning life and politics in the Cayman Islands were made by the governor of Jamaica. Less than a week after that crucial meeting, the first Legislative Assembly for the Cayman Islands was elected. In 1835, the Declaration of Emancipation freeing local slaves was read from the front steps of the house. But in 1877 tragedy struck when one of the daughters of the house was killed by a bolt of lightning. So grief-stricken were the rest of the family that they chose to move out of their home, and it sat vacant for the next 100 years.

In 1991 the Cayman Islands government purchased the house and surrounding property, declaring it a national landmark. They began a restoration process that cost over US$7 million and took more than seven years to complete. Today, it is in magnificent shape and is one of the most visited attractions on the island.

Bodden Town

Back out on the highway, the road passes through **Newlands**, where pastures grazed by cattle and goats dot the landscape. About 3 miles (5 km) farther to the east it eases into **Bodden Town**. Once the capital city of the Cayman Islands, Bodden Town is rich in history and has a number of compelling sites. The town is said to have had one of the first wells ever dug on the island and was the main source of potable water for many early settlers. It was first developed by the oldest family in the Cayman Islands, the Bodden clan, and was originally called South Side. In 1773, a map-maker started using the new name because of the number of families called Bodden he found residing in the area. In 1800 the town was a bustling community with 375 residents, but soon afterward it slipped to second-class status when development started in George Town.

The earliest and the most prominent of the Boddens was William Bodden, who served as the chief magistrate and as major general of the island's militia from 1798 until his death in 1823. Bodden was fondly called the Grand Old Man of Grand Cayman and is remembered for being instrumental in the building of the first roads, churches, and large schooners in Grand Cayman. Bodden is, in fact, the most common surname on the island, and in only a few days here you are bound to bump into someone who shares it. It is also the name of the district that includes Savannah and other nearby towns.

Paying tribute to British history, the first attraction of note is **Queen Victoria's Monument**. Built in 1910 by the residents of Bodden Town, in honor of

Right: an island idyll – a seat in the shade on a sandy shore

the late queen, the monument was often used during the 1920s and 1930s for open-air community meetings of local men who congregated here to discuss politics, sport, and island news. Not far away are **Guard House Park** and **Gun Square**. With an adjacent parking lot, the Guard House was originally built for protection against pirates and the Spanish marauders who often tried to invade the island from the nearby shore. It also provided shelter for the military men who watched over the area. What remains of the original house is an old stone wall, a memorial plaque with historic information about the site, and two cannons that point in the direction of the sea. Nearby

Gun Square used to be the site of a small but strategically important British fort that guarded the town.

A short walk eastward from Gun Square is **Meagre Bay Pond**, which was used in the early 1900s as a hunting area by local people who came here to shoot duck and teal. These days it's a popular bird-watching spot and nature sanctuary because hunting in the area is now illegal and many migratory waterfowl have begun using it as a base. Early in the morning and late in the afternoon, people come here to watch the hundreds of herons, egrets, cormorants, ibis, stilts, teals, and willets that gather to feed.

Situated behind the Gun Square, **Mission House** is another historic building in the Bodden district. Built in the 1840s by slave labor, Mission House is a classic wattle and daub structure that was used by Christian missionaries to the islands. Last on the list of echoes from the past in the town is the **Slave Wall**. It can be found at the end of Old Monument Road and is marked by a small historic sign. Sometimes referred to as Drummond's Wall, named in memory of the slave who supervised its construction, this old stone wall

Top: enjoying a cool drink with daddy
Above: on one of the walkways at Rum Point

was built some time in the early 1800s for protection from attackers, and was originally several miles long. A few sections of it remain intact, but most of it has been worn down by storms or ravaged by scavengers who stole the valuable stones to build their own homes nearby.

A Perfect End

The perfect way to end a day trip along the Southeast Coast is to stop for dinner at the **Lighthouse Restaurant** (tel: 947 2047), just a few miles east of Bodden Town in an area called Breakers. One of the most scenic restaurants on the island, the Lighthouse is a local landmark, with elegant indoor seating along with a dining space on a verandah that hangs right out over the sea. The sound of waves crashing onto the shore mingles with the strains of the classical music that is always playing in the background. Decorated with nautical artifacts and photos of striking lighthouses from around the world, the restaurant serves Italian and seafood specialties such as shrimp and lobster sautéed in olive oil, pesto *focaccia* bread with shaved parmesan cheese, thick lasagnas, wood-roasted salmon, and an assortment of Italian pastries and cheesecakes.

5. WEST END *(see map, p40)*

A drive through the laid-back residential neighborhood of West End, on the North Shore, with stops at Caribbean Charlie's, Rum Point, Cayman Kai, and Booby Cay.

Although there is a convenient ferry that takes passengers from the Seven Mile Beach area to Rum Point in West End, the long drive that begins in George Town is worth the effort. If you come by car you have the option of tooling around the various neighborhoods once you arrive, rather than being stranded in one spot. And slowly winding past the string of funky beach houses that line the North Shore, you get an immediate sense of a casual community where the vehicles of choice are beat-up old jeeps rather than modern, air-conditioned sedans. Lacking the razzle-dazzle of more highly-developed tourist areas nearer George Town, this area of Grand Cayman is far more mellow, down-to-earth, and easy to enjoy.

Departing from downtown George Town, drive east on South Sound Road until it turns in to Red Bay Road, and continue east along the coast until you get to Frank Sound. Here, turn left onto Queen's Highway, the only road that dissects the island. Continue along this road, past Queen Elizabeth II Botanic Park, several cow pastures, and not much else until it ends on the northern coast. Once here, you can take off in either direction and explore the most secluded and least populated part of Grand Cayman. Many of the homes here have jokey names hanging on signs out front – *Time Out, No Big Ting, Paradise Found, Ho Hum, Happy to be Home.*

Right: a sleek yacht in the waters of Cayman Kai

Caribbean Charlie

Just a few miles west of Queen's Highway on North Shore Road, a tiny wooden signpost that is easy to miss points the way to **Caribbean Charlie's** (tel: 947 9453). After winding down a bumpy dirt road, you reach the inland neighborhood officially known as **Hutland**. It is said to have got its name from the numerous small huts that were built here by local farmers in the late 19th century. Smack in the middle of Hutland, and surrounded by fruit trees, a whimsical little cottage with gingerbread trim and a tropical garden comes into view and you know that you have arrived.

Charlie Ebanks and his wife, Elaine, are usually inside hard at work, but quickly appear to greet visitors. A native-born Caymanian artist still practicing a dying art form, Charlie has become world famous for his hand-made wooden birdcages that are often sold before they're even completed. Painted in bright colors – lizard green, shocking pink, Caribbean blue, sunburst yellow – the cages are each uniquely designed replicas of homes and historic buildings in the Cayman Islands, and come with a registration number and certificate of ownership.

Charlie travels away from the island several times a year to collect the wood he uses; types range from teak to mahogany and pine. Since the 1980s, fans of his work have been stopping by to add more and more pieces to their personal collections. Along with the cages, Charlie also produces custom-made furniture, wall plaques, towel racks, knick knacks, and warri boards, used for playing a

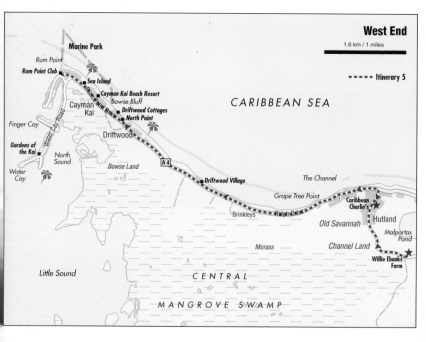

checkers-like game, which originated in Africa and today is common in the Caribbean. And each night at about sundown, Charlie and his New Jersey-born wife crank up the reggae, break out the rum, and start dancing in the middle of their shop. Just the chance to meet the two of them makes the drive to the West End well worthwhile.

Not far from Caribbean Charlie's, and also in Hutland, Willie Ebanks (Charlie's brother) runs a pig farm that oddly enough attracts many visitors, although it's not your average tourist destination. Along with tending to his hogs, Willie has taken it upon himself to protect and feed a large flock of West Indian whistling ducks that now call his property home. A protected species that was becoming more and more rare in the Cayman Islands, the whistling ducks are now abundant, thanks to Willie Ebanks. On a small pond behind his house, hundreds of these birds – they actually do whistle rather than quack – start congregating late in the afternoon and then line up, patiently waiting for Willie to bring them their evening meal.

Rum Point to Booby Cay

Heading farther west on North Shore Road will take you right into **Rum Point**. Legend has it that back in the old pirate days, a ship loaded with hundreds of bottles of rum sank off-shore from this spot and that's how it got its name. A small peninsula of land that sits under a dense canopy of casuarina and Australian pine trees, Rum Point is a lively commercial enclave of sun decks, wooden walk-ways, restaurants, bars, gift shops, picnic tables, hammocks, and a broad, white beach that is popular with local families and young people. Visitors here take it easy, loll around in the sun, and just enjoy the view. Along with a very relaxed atmosphere, water-sports are the main draw here and several operators offer windsurf boards, hobie cats, small sailboats, bicycles, and snorkeling equipment for rent, as well as trips in glass-bottomed boats.

Just a bit to the south of Rum Point is **Cayman Kai**, a residential neighborhood of plush waterfront homes with million-dollar price tags, and the **Cayman Kai Beach Resort**. Kai means by the sea, and this entire area is enveloped in the salty scent of the ocean. Many people come here to bicycle, jog, or just stroll through the beautiful neighborhood.

A little farther to the south is **Booby Cay**, a protected bird sanctuary nestled inside **North Sound**. About 30 sq. miles (78 sq. km) in diameter, North Sound is a region of mangrove swamps and small mangrove islands that are ideal nesting spots for birds, especially the boobies that roost here year round. Other birds likely to be spotted include herons, egrets, ospreys,

Left: building castles in the sand
Above: if you venture too close to the Blow Holes you will get drenched

ducks, and frigates. It is also a favorite spot for kayakers who come to poke around the channels cut into the dense mangroves, and listen to the sounds of the birds. Only about 15 ft (5 m) deep, the waters of North Sound are crystal clear and almost always calm.

6. EAST END   *(see map below)*

An afternoon drive to the East End of the island with visits to the Blow Holes, Goring Bluff Lighthouse, Gun Bay, and the Memorial to the Wreck of the Ten Sails.

East of Bodden Town and past Frank Sound, the coastal highway meanders through the district of **East End**, a delightful area of quiet beaches, wind-blown trees, busy fishing boats, quaint Caymanian cottages, and small, family-run stores. One of the prettiest beaches in this area is **Heritage Beach**, a small public area maintained by the National Trust. The oldest continuously settled community on the island, East End was founded in the late 17th century by Isaac Bodden, and the district is still sometimes referred to as **Old Isaac's**, its original name. Isaac was the grandson of William Bodden, one of the first settlers to make his home in Grand Cayman *(see page 37)*.

Near the shore, just before the village limits of East End, you will spot the **Blow Holes**, a natural attraction in one of the most scenic spots on the

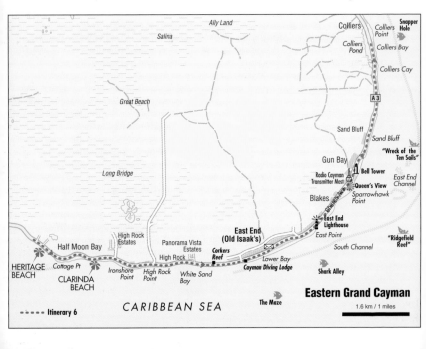

Eastern Grand Cayman

1.6 km / 1 miles

- - - - - Itinerary 6

grand cayman

island. A small sign marks the point where a series of steps leads down to the coast. Usually, however, visitors locate the Blow Holes by the sound they make, as a rushing blast of water shoots geyser-like through the rugged iron-shore stone. The water spouts tend to shoot out in bursts of three or four at a time, followed by a lull. If you get too close, you're sure to wind up soaking wet. Created by thousands of years of crashing surf weathering away the iron-shore that juts out from the coast, the holes and caves that make up this spot are a favorite hang-out of local teenagers who come here to watch the show and drink chilled coconut water, sold by a seaside vendor.

A bit farther down the highway the **East End Lighthouse** appears, perched atop Goring Bluff. For centuries, there have been lighthouses on this part of the coast. One of the first was simply a large lantern hoisted up a 75-ft (23-m) ship's mast, followed by a more substantial one using a kerosene lamp, that was built in 1912. The coastal road didn't extend this far until 1935, and before that most people arrived here by boat. The current lighthouse, built in 1937, is solar-powered; it still functions as the main navigation marker for this end of the island. A few years ago the Cayman Islands National Trust built a pretty park around it, laid out with walkways, a flower garden, and an array of medicinal plants of the kind grown by early settlers.

Less than a mile from the Lighthouse is **Gun Bay**, a small town that was first settled in the 1800s. At the time, Gun Bay was one of two legal entry points to the Cayman Islands and the community that lived here was responsible for controlling the maritime traffic, trading with passing ships, and registering all the births, deaths, and marriages that took place in the East End.

A Maritime Disaster

The most significant thing about Gun Bay is that it was the site of the **Wreck of the Ten Sails**, and several monuments mark the spot of the most tragic maritime accident in Cayman Islands' history. A look-out point called Queen's View also stands by the shore, and a huge anchor that can be spotted jutting out of the water just offshore is said to have belonged to one of the sunken ships.

It was here, in the early morning hours of February 8, 1794, that 10 British merchant ships were swept off course by strong winds and thrust into the treacherous coral reef. Part of a convoy of 58 merchant vessels escorted by a British Navy frigate, HMS *Convert*, the ships had left Jamaica two days earlier and were en route for Britain. Just after midnight, the *Convert* was overtaken by some of the convoy's ships, and a few hours later gunfire erupted. Amid the confusion, the captain, John Lawford, realized he had sailed too close to some coral reefs, and in an effort to warn the rest of the convoy he hoisted his sails. Unfortunately, the captains of the other ships

Left: water-sports at the Tortuga Club
Right: serious domino players at Pirates' Cove Bar

took this as a sign that they were being attacked by pirates and should move closer to shore. In a matter of minutes, disaster struck. With churning seas, strong winds, and little moonlight to guide them, all 10 vessels crashed into the reef and ran aground.

The rough water and gusty winds prevented most of the islanders' boats from coming to the rescue. It was the daring effort of a few local fishermen who rowed out to the wrecks that saved hundreds of sailors who were flailing around in the water and clinging to the sinking ships. When it was all over, eight people were dead, but maritime historians agree that the death toll could easily have been much higher. The valiant effort of the Caymanian rescuers so impressed King George III, it is said, that he granted the Cayman Islands 'freedom from taxation in perpetuity.' Britain and America were at odds because the Americans had just declared independence, and their president, George Washington, is said to have shed no tears over the accident.

The Wreck of the Ten Sails became one of the most talked-about events in Cayman Islands' history, and inspired several books and legends. Some of the tales were false, including one claiming that Prince William, the future William IV, was on board one of the vessels. These days, the waters around Gun Bay are among the most visited dive sites in Grand Cayman. Many people come here from all over the world to catch a glimpse of the eerie relics of the ships, eight of which remain, sitting like ghosts under the sea.

Past the Memorial to the Wreck of the Ten Sails, the highway curves round the corner of the island past Sand Bluff and on to Colliers Bay.

7. SUBMARINE TOUR *(see pullout map)*

A choice of underwater tours that are particularly recommended for those who do not like diving or scuba-diving.

A submarine tour is a great alternative to diving as it allows non-divers to see the delights of the underwater world safely and comfortably without ever get-

ting their faces wet. Several operators offer the trips, and they are all located in George Town. Most of the following day-time submarine tours depart on the hour all day long. Evening tours are scheduled three night a week. Reservations for all the tours are suggested, especially during the busy winter months.

First on the list is **Atlantis Adventures** (tel: 949 7700; approximately US$75). This company offers more than 10 tours a day, with departures from near the cruise-ship dock in George Town harbor. They use 48-passenger submarines that are spacious, air-conditioned and surprisingly comfortable. Passengers are ferried out to the submarine in an open-top boat and then climb one-by-one down the hatch via a narrow ladder. Inside, the cabin has a long row of seats down the middle,

Left: a tour guide provides information on board an Atlantis submarine

grand cayman

each facing outward, and the atmosphere feels very similar to that in the interior of an airplane.

Once the doors are sealed, the submarine slowly drops 100 ft (30 m) down the face of the Cayman wall to the ocean floor, while a tour guide explains what can be seen outside. The only other sounds to be heard are the 'oohs' and 'ahhs' of the passengers, and the gentle hum of the engines as the pilot navigates the ship. Sitting single file, passengers have their own portholes that afford amazing sights – intricate corals, sponge gardens, exotic marine creatures, and tropical fish within inches of the thick glass windows. Occasionally, scuba divers swim by the submarine and feed fish or wave. The air pressure inside the cabin feels totally natural, and the experience is not at all claustrophobic. Laminated information cards detailing the types of fish in the water hang beside each porthole and make for useful reference. Although most of the tours only visit the reef off the harbor, others venture farther out to take a look at sunken ships. Atlantis also offers night tours when the submarine's lights guide the craft along and reveal an entirely different world that only comes to life after dark.

For a peek at the sea without being fully submerged, both the **Nautilus Undersea Tour** (tel: 945 1355) and the **Seaworld Explorer Semi-Submarine Tour** (tel: 949 7700) offer one-hour day-time trips in ships with glass hulls that enable passengers to sit 6 ft (2 m) below the water's surface in a glass observatory. Located at George Town harbor, these two tours are especially good for small children, who might be frightened by the real submarine trip, and for those who worry about getting claustrophobic. While they don't have such interesting views as the deeper submarine tours, they do provide a taste of what lies below the surface.

Down to the Depths

The most fascinating and adventurous of the Grand Cayman submarine trips is the **Deep Explorer Tour** (tel: 949 7700; approximately US$350–$450 depending on the time of year). An authentic research vessel used by the National Geographic Society and other scientific organizations, this submarine is available for passenger use only in the Cayman Islands. The two-passenger vessel is about the size of a helicopter with two seats in the forward section; the pilot sits directly behind the passengers. Compressed air tanks, ballast, and high-powered batteries hang from the bottom of the craft. The procedure is similar to that on the other submarine trips – passengers are ferried out to the sub and then climb inside. This one, however, is much, much smaller, more confining, and not air-conditioned, so it's definitely not for those who suffer from claustrophobia.

Above: visitors try out a submarine while still on dry land

Gently, it drops down to about 1,000 ft (305 m) below the surface. Unlike the larger submarines that constantly move backward and forward, the *Deep Explorer* does not undertake much horizontal movement and most of the trip is purely vertical.

What passengers get to see is a layer-cake of marine life that changes drastically as the vessel descends deeper, and encompasses several different marine zones that range from light, bright coral reefs, to a spooky moonscape terrain when you get closer to the edge of the Cayman Trench. Down at 1,000 ft (305 m), there really isn't much marine life to see except for bizarre-looking fish with very large eyes, and six-gill sharks that live only in the deep, but the experience of having gone down to such depths (something few people have ever done) is what the appeal of this trip is all about.

Cozy Option

While it only goes down to about 100 ft (30 m), a more cozy tour option is a ride on the *Seamobile* with **Cayman Submarines** (tel: 916 3483). These small submarines also take only two passengers at a time, and have pilots wearing dive gear who ride on the outside of the vessel and navigate from behind and outside the passenger compartment while giving a narrated tour at the same time. Featuring personalized tours with a totally unobstructed view from the cabin, Cayman Submarines are willing to take passengers whereever they wish to go – down the face of the Cayman Wall, to specific dive sites, or to sunken ships. They will also chase after sharks, stingrays, or turtles if you ask them to.

For all the submarine trips – day or night, shallow or deep – passengers should note that a camera flash is useless because it reflects off the glass portholes, and only film with an ASA rating of 1,000 is capable of capturing the images of the deep.

Above: descending a narrow ladder into the submarine's interior

8. THE BOTANIC PARK AND MASTIC TRAIL *(see map, p48)*

Spend a morning exploring the lush tropical gardens of Queen Elizabeth II Botanic Park with an option to hike through the Mastic Trail.

While few people pack hiking boots when they go to Grand Cayman, they do come in handy for a trek through the wilder regions of the island. It's a good idea to make this trip in the morning before the sun gets too strong. Even then, be sure to lather on the sunblock, wear a hat, and spray yourself liberally with mosquito repellent. For a thorough look round, plan on scheduling a few hours for the visit.

Located in the deep interior of the island, **Queen Elizabeth II Botanic Park** (daily 9am–6.30pm; admission fee; tel: 947 9462) is a 65-acre (26-ha) nature preserve that offers visitors a glimpse of what the island was like before tourism came to town. Several tour operators offer trips to the park, or you can make the 45-minute drive from George Town by taking Red Bay Road and continuing east along the coast until you get to Frank Sound.

Here, turn left onto Queen's Highway and a few miles along a sign points to a wide, paved road lined with towering palms and the park entrance.

This is the Cayman Islands' premier show garden, a masterpiece of nature that came to life in 1991 after hundreds of volunteers (including school children and prisoners) spent thousands of hours clearing the land, surveying the area, and identifying and documenting trees and plants. In 1993 it won *Islands* magazine's Ecotourism Award for the finest ecotourism project in the Caribbean. Although it had been in existence for a few years, the park was 'officially' opened by Queen Elizabeth II in 1994, during her second visit to the Cayman Islands. More recently, a modern, two-story **Visitors' Centre** was added. Equipped with a well-stocked café and gift shop, it offers plenty of information about the park. It also has interpretive exhibits that explain the flora and fauna of the islands, and occasionally hosts lectures and demonstrations. An informative exhibit in the park describes the island's many poisonous plants, such as maiden plum, which has a sap similar to poison ivy, and machineel, a plant with an extremely toxic and irritating sap.

According to Park Director, Andrew Guthrie, about 50 percent of Grand Cayman's 678 species of indigenous plants are found growing naturally in the park, and there is also a host of colorful bird and animal life. The preserve also contains several species of rare plants found nowhere else in the world. The clearly-marked **Woodland Trail** guides hikers through about 1 mile (2 km) of dense woodland with

Above: exotic flora in the Queen Elizabeth II Botanic Park
Right: a lot of watering is necessary to keep the vegetation in good shape

a series of panels offering information about the plants. The natural habitats change about every 100 yards (91 m), depending on the type of soil and the elevation, and include wetlands, cactus thickets, logwood swamps, air-plant woodlands, thatch-palm hammocks, and tall mahogany forests. Not far from the trail, wild orchids and bromeliads thrive in a small pool fed by a buttonwood swamp.

Inside the park is a 2-acre (0.8-ha), man-made lake whose lily-pond areas are home to many native aquatic birds, including a large flock of whistling ducks, herons, stilts, coots, teals, and egrets. Originally part of the adjacent swamp, the brackish water lake is only about 3 ft (1 m) deep, but has three small islands in the center, with native vegetation.

Flowers, Heritage, and Iguanas

Overlooking the lake is the outrageously beautiful **Floral Colour Garden**, a 2.5-acre (1-ha) patch of land with hundreds of varieties of exotic, flowering plants, native and foreign, that bloom year round. Arranged according to color, the flower patches slide through the rainbow from pink to red to orange, then yellow to blue and purple. Many of these plants are used for research as well as being part of a cooperative propagation program for botanists in other parts of the Caribbean. Nearby is a cascading waterfall that flows from a freshwater pond where dozens of turtles live, and a little tea house that serves refreshments.

The most recent addition, and perhaps the most interesting aspect of the park, is the 2-acre (0.8-ha) **Heritage Garden**. The centerpiece is a perfectly-restored wooden cottage, brought here from East End in 1995. An excellent example of classic Caymanian architecture, the pastel-painted cottage is furnished with antiques and includes a wide front porch, a cook room, a cistern, and a well, all reminiscent of life on the island 100 years ago. Originally, the three-room structure was home to a Caymanian family with nine children. Along with a traditional sand yard, it has a small garden full of plants commonly found in early gardens, such as crotons, lilies, cat claws, tea bushes, and medicinal plants and herbs such as aloe vera.

There is an abundance of Cayman blue iguanas wandering around the garden. As part of an island-wide effort by the National Trust to protect the endemic Cayman blue, the park has implemented a breeding program that collects the iguanas from other parts of the islands then releases them here. About 30 of them have been placed in a breeding pen on the property, that is also used to

Queen Elizabeth II Botanic Park

Entrance/Exit

Restrooms, Drinking Fountain, First Aid

Nursery and Plant Shop

Maintenance Office

Iguana Habitat

Woodland Trail

Ticket Booth

Queen Elizabeth II Monument

Visitors Parking

Woodland Trail Entrance

Visitors' Centre (Botanic Park Gift Shop, Public Telephone, Lost & Found)

Cafe

Woodland Trail

Heritage Garden

Floral Colour Garden

Gazebo   Lake and Wetlands

Restrooms   Drinking Fountain

Map drawn with permission from the Queen Elizabeth II Botanic Park

conduct scientific research. In addition to the iguanas, there are tree frogs, lizards, and harmless snakes in the garden.

The Mastic Trail

If a hike through the Botanic Park does not satisfy your appetite for nature, you could visit the **Mastic Trail**. Located on the west side of Queen's Highway, a few miles from the Botanic Park, the trail is not easily accessible and it is usually necessary to hire a local guide. The office of the National Trust for the Cayman Islands in George Town (tel: 949 0045) arranges escorted morning and afternoon tours, as does a company called **Silver Thatch Excursions** (tel: 945 6588). Both provide transportation to and from the trail, as well as cold drinks along the way. Silver Thatch is owned by Geddes Hislop, a Caymanian-born biologist trained in Canada, who was involved in the formation of the Queen Elizabeth II Botanic Park. His tours are highly regarded by nature lovers and are considered the best in the Cayman Islands.

First created over 200 years ago, when residents of the North Shore area used it as a source of timber for export and building materials, and used thereafter as the route for herding cattle across the island, the Mastic Trail traverses one of the last tracts of primary evergreen woodland left on Grand Cayman. It gets its name from the giant mastic trees that grow naturally on the land. Before roads were built in the area, the Mastic Trail was used for many years as a thoroughfare, and after the roads were built it became overgrown. In 1994 the National Trust for the Cayman Islands adopted it as a pet restoration project. The Trust cleared the path, and a year later reopened it as an attraction for visitors interested in the island's vegetation and its past.

A traditional footpath that cuts through from the interior to the island's north shore, it winds for several miles through ancient, dry woodlands, mangrove swamps, rock formations, and farming areas. It also contains what is jokingly referred to as 'the mountain,' a rise of dirt which, at 60 ft (18 m) above sea level is the highest point in Grand Cayman. Dense and rugged and teeming with birds, it contains over 100 species of trees and more than 500 species of plants, and has a distinctly primeval atmosphere that enables you to imagine what the island looked like 1,000 years ago. Wild banana orchids are often in full bloom, and because it is so thick with plant life, it feels like a tunnel with only brief rays of sunlight passing through.

Above: a vivid hibiscus bloom
Right: exploring the Woodland Trail

9. DIVING IN GRAND CAYMAN *(see pullout map)*

A round-up of choices for exploring the best dive spots around Grand Cayman, including Orange Canyon, Trinity Caves, the Cali Wreck, Bat's Cave, and the Wreck of the Ten Sails.

Since the 1950s, Grand Cayman has been a large gold star on the map of the world's greatest scuba destinations, and advanced divers often describe the underwater experience here as addictive. Dramatic wall diving (around a reef wall or drop off), phenomenal visibility, womb-like water temperatures, breathtaking marine life, historic shipwrecks, and a dive industry with a long reputation for responsibility – Grand Cayman has it all.

The exhilarating underwater atmosphere has raised the awareness, among Caymanians and those abroad, of the islands' role as a scuba destination. World-renowned scuba diver Jean-Michel Cousteau (son of Jacques) is the official spokesperson for Cayman Islands' scuba diving and snorkeling. 'I look forward to helping the Cayman Islands continue their tradition of marine protection and to be a model for other destinations around the world,' said Cousteau. Along with promoting scuba diving, Cousteau plays a large part in the local decision-making process regarding environmental protection, sustainable tourism, and responsible water-sports.

To appreciate how amazing the diving is you should try it. But you can't just strap on a tank and dive in. Recreational diving is regulated worldwide by several independent organizations including PADI, NAUI, and SSI, and you must have proof that you've passed at least a basic dive course before any operator will take you aboard. Fortunately for novices, dozens of programs are available throughout Grand Cayman and the other islands that offer a variety of instructional scuba lessons, ranging from one-day scuba resort courses to master level four-day certification classes.

Be aware that strict marine park laws are enforced in the Cayman Islands, and all divers are expected to utilize dive flags or markers, must never remove anything from the water, and must not go deeper than 100 ft (30 m).

Above: setting off for a dive excursion

Although scuba diving is the best way to really experience the thrill of being underwater in the Cayman Islands, there are also many places where the snorkeling is divine. Most scuba guidebooks list hundreds of designated dive sites around Grand Cayman, so the list of choices can be overwhelming. A few of the sites, however, are considered unmissable by many experienced divers, and the following is a round-up of some of those favorite spots to which people return time after time.

West Coast, George Town, and Southern Sites

Starting off on the west side of the island, which is protected from the trade winds, the area near West Bay is like a salt-water swimming pool. One of the most vivid sites here is **Orange Canyon**. With visibility exceeding 100 ft (30 m), this deep site fairly close to the beach is a spectacular kaleidoscope of bright orange, elephant-ear sponges, coral pinnacles, and a narrow cave. Nearby is **Trinity Caves**, a coral mass that slopes down the edge of the wall through a series of chimneys, arches, and gullies. Three main canyons alternate, with ridges dropping from about 50 ft (15 m) on the top of the reef to almost 100 ft (30 m), and are marked by black corals, deep-water sea fans, lobster, shrimp, and a variety of fish.

About 50 yds (45 m) away from Trinity Caves is **Cemetery Beach Reef**. Located off a waterfront cemetery, this patch reef lies in less than 10 ft (3 m) of water very close to shore and is marked by elkhorn corals and hundreds of fish that like to be fed by hand.

A bit to the south near Seven Mile Beach is **Paradise Reef**, a shallow dive with little or no current. Here, lots of sea fans, sea plumes, and friendly fish are the main draw. Adjacent to Paradise is the ***Oro Verde* Wreck**, the first man-made dive site ever created in Grand Cayman. This 181-ft (55-m) ship was intentionally sunk here in 1980 – before that, it is said to have been used by drug smugglers. Now it lies on its port side with the bow facing north. Although broken up quite a bit by winter storms, it is covered with marine life, including garden eels, grouper, snapper, and crabs.

Offshore from George Town are the ***Cali* Wreck** and the ***Balboa***. The Cali is a shallow dive with a maximum depth of 20 ft (6 m). Sunk here in 1944, the *Cali* was a 220-ft (67-m) four-masted schooner that was blown up by the British Corps of Army Engineers in 1957. It is now scattered in pieces on the ocean floor, but its winches, boilers, and hull plates are all recognizable. Since it is very close to the surface, many snorkelers, as well as scuba divers, visit

Above: a diver at the reef off George Town
Right: fire coral wafting in the water

this site. A bit farther out than the *Cali* is the *Balboa*, a 375-ft (114-m) lumber steamer that was wrecked off George Town during a hurricane in 1932. Like the *Cali*, it was blown up because it was a navigation hazard, and is now strewn over a wide area. Both the *Cali* and the *Balboa* are filled with marine life, and are often used as night dive sites.

Not far away is the **Wreck of the *Gamma***, an old freighter that has been sitting on the ocean floor here for decades. The ship's rusty, orange-colored hull is half exposed and half submerged and presents a striking view. Shore access is easy from a coral cove, and the submerged part of the ship serves as home to many varieties of fish.

Also near George Town is **Devil's Grotto**, a shallow dive marked by a single-pin mooring buoy on the south side of the reef. A very popular spot, the Grotto is full of gullies and crevices with lots of tarpon swimming around. Nearby is **Parrot's Reef**, another shallow dive, directly offshore from South Church Street. An excellent spot for underwater photography, it is often used as a training dive site and, along with coral heads, includes the remains of a small tugboat used as an *Atlantis* submarine tender, which sank during a storm in 1987. A little bit south of Parrot's Reef is **Waldo's Reef**. Named in honor of its most famous resident, a moray eel known as Waldo, this shallow site is filled with numerous tame fish and a bunch of barracuda.

Moving along the south side of the island we come to **Oriental Gardens** and **Chinese Gardens**, both just offshore on the outskirts of George Town. Shallow dives marked by a single-pin mooring buoy, they are lovely sites with acres of brightly-colored staghorn coral, sea plumes, soft corals, and schooling fish.

Also in this area is **Dangerous Dan Drop-Off**, a deep and dramatic dive. A large coral buttress cut with ravines and under-hanging coral gardens, Dangerous Dan's is swarming with marine life, including lots of spotfin hogfish. Not far away is **Bat's Cave**, an intricate and extensive tunnel and cave system with a profusion of elkhorn coral and lots of lobsters and shrimp.

East End and the North

Off the East End of Grand Cayman is the most famous site in all the Cayman Islands, the **Wreck of the Ten Sails** *(see page 43)*. Here, the somber remains of 10 British merchant ships that sank in 1794 attract divers from around the world and offer a haunting glimpse of Caymanian maritime history. Although not as dramatic, another popular site fairly close to the Ten Sails is **The Maze**. A deep dive that often has choppy currents, The Maze features a honeycomb of tunnels with several swim-throughs that meander into

Left: a Caribbean reef shark swims through the deep blue waters

dark caves and fissures and then out again into light blue seas. Two resident bull sharks are a common sight, as are black coral fans, deep-water gorgonian fans, and dense formations of brain coral.

A few miles north east of The Maze is **Shark Alley**, a deep dive prone to rip tides from the channel. Although it is considered very difficult, Shark Alley can make for an exciting dive, due to the many large boulders, coral buttresses, small caves, and pristine sponges. Also in the East End is *Ridgefield* **Reef**, a shallow site prone to currents. The *Ridgefield* was a 441-ft (144-m) Liberian freighter weighing over 7,000 tons/tonnes that ran aground here in 1962. Today, it is almost entirely coated with algae, corals, sea fans, and marine life. The last place of note in this part of the island is **Snapper Hole**, one of the top dive sites in Grand Cayman. A shallow dive with good visibility, Snapper Hole has an amazing mass of large caves and fissures inside the reef's structure. It's a fascinating spot, full of coral growth and tropical fish, and has a rusty old anchor embedded in the top of the reef.

Along the northern coast of Grand Cayman, the underwater atmosphere is world famous for its sheer drop-off points with higher than average visibility. A few of the more popular sites include **Haunted House**, a deep dive to the east of Rum Point Channel. What looks like a large amphitheater is formed out of two coral buttresses and is covered in coral trees, black barrel sponges, turtles, and rays. **No Name Wall**, a deep dive with moderate currents, is noted for a series of four perpendicular ravines that plunge over the wall. Not far from No Name is **Chinese Wall**, a canyon with a cave-like opening that has three large buttress formations, and a profusion of black coral, sponges, trumpet fish, grouper, snapper, and tiny shrimp. In the east, close to Old Man Bay is **Babylon**, a series of ravines with brilliant rope sponges, pristine corals, and large schools of fish. Heading west toward Morgans Harbor, you come to **Ghost Mountain**, a deep dive for intermediate to advanced divers. Noted for its large coral pinnacle lying in a sand slope at about 140 ft (43 m), Ghost Mountain is almost always full of large schools of fish.

Above: stop-light parrot fish swim among bluehead wrasse coral

Cayman Brac

O ne of the two 'little sisters' of the Cayman Islands, Cayman Brac is 89 miles (143 km) northeast of Grand Cayman. Twelve miles (19 km) long by 1 mile (1.6 km) wide, it has a resident population of about 1,600 and topographically is the most interesting of the islands. Brac is the Gaelic word for bluff, and the island's rugged limestone bluff that dominates the interior rises to 140 ft (43 m), marked by honey-combed caves and a fascinating array of vegetation.

Far less developed than Grand Cayman, Cayman Brac is made up of a friendly, close-knit community of people known as Brackers, most of whom

are descendants of Caymanian seafarers. It also has a small but solid ex-pat community of people who have fallen in love with the peace and quiet of the island, and the quality of life it affords them.

Until the mid-1960s there were only 10 phone lines on the island, and electricity didn't appear until 1966. Although there has been a modest amount of development in the past 10 years, Cayman Brac is still a place where people never lock their doors, and motorists wave to each other as they pass. Although it is small in size, it has every amenity a visitor could want, including good hotels, fine restaurants, and plenty of fun things to explore. There's even a small hospital, in case of emergency.

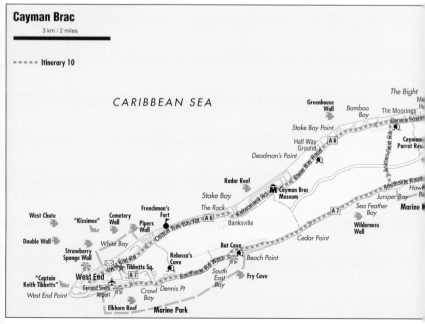

Cayman Brac

3 km / 2 miles

- - - - **Itinerary 10**

CARIBBEAN SEA

The Bight

Greenhouse Wall   Bamboo Bay   The Moorings

Stake Bay Point   Dennis Foster

Half Way Ground   A6   Cayman Parrot Res.

Deadman's Point

Radar Reef

Stake Bay   M Cayman Brac Museum   Southside Road   Hawk

The Rock   Juniper Bay   Bay   Marine

Frenchman's Fort   Banksville   A6   A7   Sea Feather Bay

West Chute   Cemetery Wall   Pipers Wall   Wilderness Wall

"Kissimee"   Cedar Point

Double Wall   White Bay   Bat Cave

Strawberry Sponge Wall   Rebecca's Cave   Beach Point

West End   Tibbetts Sq.   A7   South East Bay   Fry Cave

"Captain Keith Tibbetts"   Southside Rd West

West End Point   Gerrard Smith Airport   Crawl Bay   Dennis Pt

Elkhorn Reef   Marine Park

Departing from the George Town airport, both Cayman Airways and Island Air *(see Practical Information, page 81 for details)* provide a 40-minute flight to Cayman Brac. The entire island can be seen in one day, but an overnight trip is suggested, especially if you want to do some diving, and renting a car for the day will enable you to explore the lesser known nooks and crannies of the island at your leisure.

10. HIGHLIGHTS OF CAYMAN BRAC *(see map below)*

An overnight trip to Cayman Brac with a hike along the bluff, and visits to the Bat Cave, NIM's Cottage, and the Cayman Brac Museum.

As soon as you land at the small **Gerard Smith Airport**, you realize you have left the intensity of Grand Cayman far behind. Tourists introduce themselves to each other, offer tips about diving in the area, and act as if they are part of a family reunion. Even the car rental agencies are casual – many don't even ask to see a driver's license.

Most of the major hotels are within minutes of the airport on the western end of the island, and after checking in, you can start your day tour. This area is also where the best beaches are and the swimming is terrific. Driving east on the one road along the coast, this stretch is called Southside Road West, you will spot, on the left, the **Westerly Ponds**, two salt-water bodies

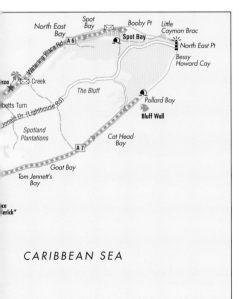

of water dotted with mangrove islands. Oblivious to the airport noise, the ponds are bird sanctuaries, home to thousands of ducks, egrets, stilts, and herons. An occasional white barn owl may be spotted, perched high in a tree. A short way past the Westerly Ponds is the **Salt Water Pond**, another marshy bird rookery, and past this a small sign points toward a gravel road leading to **Rebecca's Cave**. This large opening in the limestone bluff is the grave-site of Rebecca Bodden, a baby who died during the 1932 hurricane.

Left: local garage owner
Above: a salt-water pond

Nearby is **Bat Cave**, a large cave that has been used for over 100 years as a shelter during hurricanes. Along with most of the other caves on Cayman Brac, this one is maintained by the National Trust, and is kept in excellent condition, with guide rails and ladders to assist hikers who want to explore it. A two-level cave with wooden steps and an enormous opening, Bat Cave is very accessible and offers a panoramic view of the sea.

Continuing on for several miles, the road passes a few hotels and many private homes built right on the coast, and eventually comes to a dead end

at **Pollard Bay**. To the left, the towering bluff gradually gets higher the farther east you travel along the road. At just about any point along here you can park on the shoulder and climb up the bluff to take a short hike. There are several footpaths and trails that traverse the bluff and wind past cacti, wild orchids, and thatch palms. The green parrot is commonly seen here, as are soldier crabs and lizards.

About mid-point along this road is **Ashton Reid Road**, the island's intersection. Turn left and in about ½ mile (1 km) you will spot a gravel road that runs through the center of the island. Deep in the interior, not far from here, is the **Cayman Brac Parrot Reserve**, a 180-acre (73-ha) parcel of land designed to protect indigenous plants as well as the Cayman Brac parrot. Continue for another ½ mile (1 km) and you'll see goats and cattle in adjoining fields, and wild native plum and West Indian cherry trees growing, before you emerge on the North Shore of Cayman Brac.

NIM's Cottage

Turning right here will take you along the coast past fishing boats and small homes painted bright Caribbean colors with tin roofs and small vegetable gardens out front. Less than 1 mile (1.5 km) up the road is **La Esperanza** (tel: 948 0531), a wonderful waterfront eatery featuring authentic Caymanian cuisine. Farther along you will come to **Spot Bay** and eventually see **NIM's** (Mon–Sat 9am–7pm; tel: 948 0461), a small cottage shop and home to Tenson Scott. A native Caymanian, Scott is one of the few people on the island who is allowed to remove the caymanite stone from the bluff, and his handmade jewelry is known throughout the islands. With pick and maul, he carefully chips away the stone, and then laboriously turns it into brownish-orange masterpieces. Now in his seventies, Scott is a friendly man who can tell wonderful tales of life on Cayman Brac – and he's an experienced fisherman who can point you toward the best spots to drop a line. His shop, whose initials stand for Native Island Made, is full of his jewelry, straw hats, and local arts and crafts. Beyond NIM's the road ends at the eastern edge of the island where the rugged coastline, marked by crashing waves, is often dotted with driftwood and nautical debris.

Above: Bat Cave has always been used as a hurricane shelter, and is very accessible for those who want to explore its secrets.

cayman brac

Stake Bay

Backtracking down the coast, past the turn-off point to Ashton Reid Road, is an area of Cayman Brac known as Stake Bay, a small community that is home to the **Government Administration Building**, a duty-free store, and the small **Faith Hospita**l. A few steps away from the government offices is the **Cayman Brac Museum** (Mon–Fri 9am–noon, 1–4pm, Sat 9am–noon; free; tel: 948 2622). A white clapboard building with swing seats on the front porch, it once housed the island's post office, customs bureau, treasury, and bank, and still contains the booths of those offices.

Transformed into a museum in 1983, it now houses a large and impressive collection of artifacts and antiques that explain the island's history and offer a taste of what life was like for the early Irish, Scottish, and English settlers. Housed in glass cases, its treasures include old photographs, anchors, turtle shells, crocodile hides, hurricane lamps, wooden radios, hand-written news bulletins, carpenters' tools, sewing machines, clothing, and butter churns. It also tells the story of the brutal 1932 hurricane that killed 109 people. It just about wiped out the entire island, and still lingers in the minds of many Brackers. William Ryan, the museum's curator, is always on hand to answer questions and explain the significance of the items on display.

Leaving the museum, take the coastal road that continues to the western end of the island, toward the airport, passes a few cafés and several churches, and eventually runs into **Tibbetts Square**. A modern, strip-mall shopping center, Tibbetts Square is the island's main commercial center, where most local people come for their supplies. It includes a large, well-stocked grocery store and a cute little boutique called the **Treasure Chest**. Owned by Hyacynth Scott, a native Caymanian with family roots dating back over 100 years, the Treasure Chest sells tropical clothing, jewelry, hats, and souvenirs. Next door is **Ed's Place**, a casual watering hole where local people come to share the latest gossip.

Top: enjoy a Caymanian lunch at La Esperanza.
Right a model boat at the Cayman Brac Museum

11: DIVING IN CAYMAN BRAC *(see map, p54–5)*

This itinerary offers a few hours diving in Cayman Brac. There are several sites to choose from, including the *Tibbetts* Wreck, Strawberry Sponge Wall, the *Kissimee* Wreck, Fry Cave, and the *Prince Frederick* Wreck.

Many of the resorts on Cayman Brac have full-service dive operators on site with certified scuba masters on their staff, and are equipped with dive boats, gear, air, and anything else a visiting scuba diver might need. Most of them lead regularly-scheduled trips to various locations several times a day and once a night.

Although the dive sites off Cayman Brac are very similar to those on Grand Cayman, there are far fewer divers in the waters here. This means the coral reefs are less disturbed and therefore in better shape. It also means, in the minds of many divers, that Cayman Brac is a far more prestigious and exclusive location than Grand Cayman. There are about 50 documented dive sites scattered around the little island, and the following are just a few of the most popular.

One of the most visited and most dramatic sites is ***Tibbetts* Wreck**. A Russian destroyer intentionally sunk here in 1996 by Jean-Michel Cousteau, the MV *Captain Keith Tibbetts* is now a flagship of marine conservation. Amid a great deal of fanfare as the destroyer was sinking, Cousteau stood on the deck in full scuba gear, holding on to the guard rails as the ship gradually vanished from sight.

Over 300 ft (92 m) long and 42 ft (13 m) wide, the destroyer was part of an old Soviet fleet stationed in Cuba during the Cold War years. It was acquired by the Cayman government after the break-up of the Soviet Union, with the goal of creating an artificial reef to aid marine life in these waters. These days, it is covered in algae and other marine growth and makes for a

Above: rock beauty coral, an underwater delight

captivating dive in about 75 ft (23 m) of water off the west end of the island. Barracudas, groupers and angel fish are a familiar sight around the wreck.

Not far from Tibbetts Wreck is **Double Wall**, a deep dive with a steeply fissured reef crust and small ledge. Along with the remains of a private wreck, Double Wall has lots of fish and a profusion of sponges.

Continuing along the north coast of the west end of the island you reach **West Chute**, another deep dive, this one with very steep sand chutes, huge barrel sponges, and lots of hermit crabs and squirrel fish.

Next comes **Strawberry Sponge Wall**. As the name implies, this 75-ft (23-m) site has a lovely reef wall cut by overhangs that are adorned with beautiful strawberry vase sponges. It also has lots of starfish and thousands of garden eels.

The *Kissimee* **Wreck**, to the northeast of Sponge Wall, is a shallow dive marked by a single-pin mooring. In 1982, this retired tugboat, now sitting on her port side, was deliberately sunk to supplement the natural reef system, and is now a great favorite with photographers.

Not far away, to the east, is **Cemetery Wall**. A deep dive with deep fissures, this site is marked by large star coral, black coral, butterfly fish, and angel fish. Nearby are **Pipers Wall** and **Charlie's Reef**. Piper's has enormous canyons with pretty sea fans and black coral as well as long tube sponges. Charlie's is a shallow spot noted for its large elkhorn and staghorn corals.

South Coast Sites

Over on the opposite – south – coast is **Elkhorn Reef**, a shallow dive with four deep ridges and many gullies, canyons, and swim-throughs. It also has a huge brain coral that is almost always swarming with barracuda. **Fry Cave**, a shallow site with moderate currents, also has lots of canyons and gullies as well as plenty of arrow crabs, yellow stingrays, pistol shrimp, and crabs. Sometimes called Cio's Craig, **Wilderness Wall** is a deep dive with a moderate current. With a good reef crest and wide sandy plateau, Wilderness has some excellent coral formations, lots of chimneys cutting through the vertical wall, and coral canyons and arches.

Continuing along in an northeasterly direction, you next come to the *Prince Frederick* **Wreck**, a twin-masted, wooden-hulled schooner said to have sunk here in the latter part of the 19th century. About 100 ft (30 m) long, the wreck includes an anchor, chains, scrap metal, and lots of copper nails.

The last on the list is **Bluff Wall**, an extremely dramatic site with steep vertical drops and deep fissures, large sea fans, black coral, pink sponges, sharks, turtles, hermit crabs, and stingrays. Whichever site you choose, you are guaranteed a diving experience that will linger in your memory long after your vacation is over.

Right: a queen angel fish, one of many species that can be seen beneath the waters of Cayman Brac

Little Cayman

The baby of the Cayman Islands trio, Little Cayman is indeed little. Located 74 miles (120 km) northeast of Grand Cayman, and just 7 miles (11 km) from Cayman Brac, it is 10 miles (16 km) long by 1 mile (1.6 km) wide. A small, safe, tropical haven, Little Cayman has a resident population of about 150 people, most of whom know each other by first name. It also has one grocery store, one bank (open only on Wednesday), one small cemetery, and one school teacher, who flies in each day from Cayman Brac to preside over the education of about five local children.

In the late 1980s the island had a population of 12; there were three phone lines and no electricity. Although dozens of houses and hotels have been built since then, the National Trust has passed laws ensuring that no chain hotels or restaurants will ever come to Little Cayman. Most of the people who live here are foreigners rather than Caymanians, and they either work in the tourism industry or come to stay in their private vacation retreats.

Little Cayman's earliest visitors were pirates who used it as a base while plundering ships in nearby waters. In the early 1950s a group of American fishermen set up a camp that eventually turned into the Southern Cross Club, a popular fishing and dive resort. Today, most visitors are divers and fishermen, but the island also gets a handful of nature lovers who come to see the numerous exotic birds and more than 2,000 rock iguanas that live amid the tropical foliage. Road signs warn drivers: 'Iguanas Have the Right of Way.' All supplies on the island are either shipped in or flown in daily from George Town.

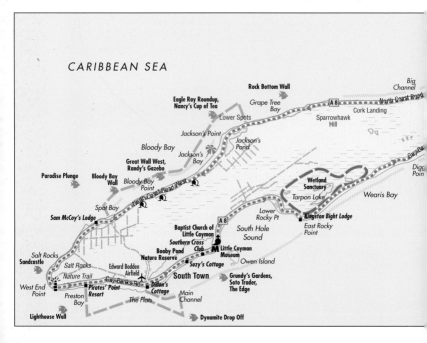

Departing from either George Town or Cayman Brac, Island Air *(see Practical Information, page 81, for details)* offers several flights a day in small propeller planes. Although the entire can be seen in a day, an overnight stay is recommended, especially if you want to do some diving. Many of the hotels provide transportation to sites around the island, and if they don't, you can rent a car or use one of the many bicycles kept at the resorts.

12. HIGHLIGHTS OF LITTLE CAYMAN *(see map below)*

An overnight trip to Little Cayman Island with visits to Booby Pond Nature Reserve, the National Trust House, and Little Cayman Museum.

The bumpy grass landing strip and one-room shack that serves as the **Edward Bodden Airfield** is the first impression that newcomers have of the island, and one that usually makes them smile. Two large iguanas live in the airport grounds, and often startle guests on their way to the public bathrooms behind the airport shack. After checking in to their resorts (most hotels collect guests from the airport), visitors can't wait to take a leisurely look round the circumference of the unspoiled island.

Less than 1 mile (1.6 km) from the airport is the **Village Square**, a tiny, strip shopping mall and so-called town center that houses the island's only

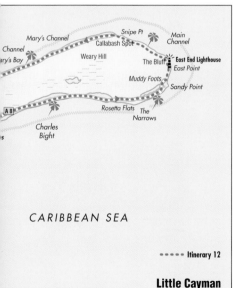

CARIBBEAN SEA

••••• Itinerary 12

Little Cayman

1.6 km / 1 mile

Above: one of over 2,000 iguanas on Little Cayman

grocery/hardware/liquor store, Internet café, bank, and newsstand. While you won't find *The New York Times* here, you will find current issues of *Caymanian Compass*, flown in daily from George Town. You can also stock up on whatever supplies you forgot to bring with you. Nearby, the **Hungry Iguana** is a terrific island-style restaurant and one of the few on Little Cayman that doesn't belong to a resort.

Owen Island

As you travel farther along the road (it's the only one, and it makes a 22-mile (35-km) loop around the entire island), several dive resorts appear along the coast, and then the paved road surface turns to packed dirt and sand. Several shallow ponds, dotted with dense foliage, can be seen on the left side of the road. Offshore in the distance you can spot **Owen Island**, sometimes called Cayman's fourth island. Owen Island used to be connected to Little Cayman by a sand spit, but that has long gone. About 230 yds (210 m) east of the shore, this 11-acre (4.5-ha) private island has a beautiful, sandy beach dotted with palms and is often used by local hotels for afternoon picnic excursions. You can also swim to the island on your own.

On the left side of the road you will spot a sign that says **Booby Pond Nature Reserve**. An inland, salt-water lagoon, Booby Pond is a United Nations-designated Ramsar wetland site over 1 mile (1.6 km) long (such sites are named after a convention in Ramsar, Iran). A few years ago a sprawling **National Trust House** was built here with a modern visitors' center, complete with a wooden walkway to the rear and high-powered telescopes for viewing birds. Inside the Trust House, museum-quality exhibits describe the flora and fauna of the island.

Above: bird-watching at Booby Pond
Right: visitors relax at Pirates Point Resort

At the back, the view of the rookery is spectacular. About 20,000 red-footed boobies live here and the commotion they cause at dusk is amazing. Carrying freshly-caught fish in their claws, they swoop in to find a perch for the night in the trees. There are also hundreds of frigate birds that circle above on the warm, thermal air currents and then join in the action. In the winter months the frigates puff up their chests and throats and do a little mating dance. In addition to the frigates and boobies, more than 150 species of resident and migratory birds can be seen on Little Cayman, including ducks, cranes, egrets, herons, and parrots. Other wildlife includes hermit crabs, turtles, frogs, and, of course, iguanas.

A few yards away and on the opposite side of the road from the National Trust House is the **Little Cayman Museum** (Mon, Wed, Thur, and Fri 3–5pm; free). In a tiny, white wooden building with lots of island character, the museum exhibits tell the stories of the colorful pirates who once camped out on the island, and the ship-building and seafaring traditions of the early settlers in the mid-19th century. Among the interesting artifacts on display are old family photographs, nautical antiques, island-made furniture, turtle shells, clothing, tools, thatch-rope, cooking utensils, household goods, and china tea cups that trace the lineage of the British royal family. A few steps north from the museum is the recently-built **Baptist Church of Little Cayman**.

Natural Habitats

Continuing on the road you will reach **Tarpon Lake**, a landlocked 15-acre (6-ha) stretch of water that attracts migratory birds and is brimming with tarpon fish. A small boardwalk leads visitors on a trail along parts of the lake's shore. The coastal road then continues round the eastern end of the island past the **East End Lighthouse** and an area called **Snipe Point**. It then heads down the northern coast, past private homes perched by the sea.

As you round the bend of the island, heading south back toward the airport, you will come to the **Salt Rocks Nature Trail**. This trail, through a dense woodland area, is thick with mahogany and palm trees, cactus bushes, and bromeliads, and passes the remains of an old railroad car that served a phosphate strip-mining plant, which once operated on the land. On Sunday morning, a local resident, Gladys Howard, leads walking tours along the trail. The owner of **Pirates Point Resort**, Howard is one of Little Cayman's most eccentric characters. A Texas-born gourmet chef and avid scuba diver, she has lived on Little Cayman since the 1980s, and is delightfully flamboyant and fun. If you can't catch her Sunday morning walk, stop off at her resort, have a drink at the bar, and invite her to regale you with tales of life on this small island.

Right: Tarpon Lake has a boardwalk running around it

13. DIVING IN LITTLE CAYMAN   *(see map, p60–61)*

A few hours' diving in the waters off Little Cayman, with a choice of spectacular sites, including the world famous Bloody Bay Wall, Paradise Plunge, Grundy's Gardens, and Soto Trader.

As on Cayman Brac, most hotels and resorts have certified scuba masters on staff and are equipped with boats, gear, air, and anything else a visiting scuba diver might need. They lead scheduled dive trips several times a day.

The waters off Little Cayman, described by the late scuba diver, Philippe Cousteau, as among the best dive sites he had ever visited, attract divers from around the world. The steep wall plunges and exquisite coral gardens around the island were what enthused Cousteau. As there is little dive traffic, the waters are almost always crystal clear. There are about 60 documented sites off Little Cayman, and a round-up of some of the more popular ones follows.

Part of the Cayman Islands Marine Park system, **Bloody Bay Wall** on the north shore is the one spot Little Cayman divers never miss. Between Jackson Point and Spot Bay, Bloody Bay has two distinct walls and over 15 recorded dive sites within it. The only wall dive in the Cayman Islands that begins its vertical leap from depths of less than 20 ft (6 m), Bloody Bay's legendary plunge has consistently clear water with visibility up to 150 ft (45 m). Local rules restrict the number of divers on each visiting boat to 20. The bay, a deep indigo abyss, is marked by winding ravines, deep crevices, coral gardens, and pristine sponges, and it is usually filled with an amazing array of marine life, including eagle rays, yellow-fin groupers, sea turtles, horse-eye jacks, parrotfish, grunts, and creole-fish.

Nearby is **Great Wall West** with a sheer and sudden drop from 18 ft (5.5 m) to more than 2,000 ft (610 m) and a bounty of yellow sea horses, lettuce-leaf plants, and reef dwellers. **Randy's Gazebo** is also near Bloody Bay Wall.

Above: coming ashore on a Little Cayman jetty

little cayman

Sometimes known as The Arch, Randy's is a deep dive with good visibility and a series of deep grooves with caves and swim-throughs, and colorful marine life.

Just south of Randy's Gazebo is **Paradise Plunge**. A single-pin buoy marks this spot, with little current on the inner reef. Here, the wall plunges in a series of overhangs covered in rope sponges and pink vase sponges. Deeper down are long sea whips and small clumps of star coral.

To the northeast of Paradise Plunge is **Eagle Ray Roundup** and **Nancy's Cup of Tea**. Eagle Ray is marked by a twin-barrel mooring buoy and contains a gentle sand slope with a natural amphitheater, usually bustling with stingrays, barjacks, eagle rays, hogfish, and snapper. In the evening, especially in summer, enormous manta rays gather in this spot and swoop and roll through the water. At Nancy's Cup, a shallow dive with good visibility, divers marvel at the huge sponges and coral heads. The site was named after Nancy Sefton, an accomplished diver who has written many articles and guides to the area. In Mary's Bay, to the north of Nancy's, is **Rock Bottom Wall**, a deep dive with a choppy surface. The coral reef wall is marked with coral pinnacle and barrel sponges.

The West Coast

Off the western tip of Little Cayman is **Sandcastle**, a deep dive with very little current. A relatively new and little-explored site, Sandcastle has lots of spur and groove formations and plenty of parrotfish. As you continue round the west coast, **Lighthouse Wall** is nearby. An exposed site, with waters that can get choppy, this is a weather-dependent dive, best done in summer. It has excellent coral formations on the reef's crest, fan corals, and lots of parrotfish. Further along is **Dynamite Drop-Off**. With a single-pin mooring buoy, Dynamite has little or no current. Large schools of snapper, grunts, and porkfish congregate here, and there is lots of finger and elkhorn coral.

Close to South Hole Sound, **Grundy's Gardens** is a deep dive with little current and excellent light for underwater photography. Named after Mike Grundy of the Cayman Islands Marine Conservation Unit, this coral buttress is usually dense with barracuda, hermit crabs, and marine worms. Next to Grundy's is **Soto Trader**, a shallow dive named after a ship that sank here in 1975 and now rests in 60 ft (18 m) of water, intact and fun to explore. Last on the list of sites, just south of Soto Trader, is **The Edge**, a deep dive with a moderate current. With good light for photography, this site is noted for its vertical wall filled with chutes and canyons and numerous species of butterfly fish.

Top: the evocatively-named stop-light parrotfish
Right: some people like to bring their own marine life with them

Leisure Activities

SHOPPING

There are two things that sum up the shopping scene in the Cayman Islands: it is **duty-free** and there is **no sales tax**. The islands boast about being a shoppers' haven and purchasing is certainly a favorite activity for many visitors. This does not, however, always translate into bargains. Since most retail items are shipped in from other countries, and are then levied with import duties, the prices of goods can be steep. It's wise, therefore, to know the cost of high-priced items back home before plopping down the credit card. Also, prices in most stores are listed in Cayman Islands dollars, so remember to factor in the exchange rate.

The range of goods found here is wide – designer clothing, china, crystal, porcelain, perfumes, leather goods, liquor, Irish linens, jewelry, cameras, Cuban cigars, antique coins, and vintage maps. Aside from these, a few local products are worth checking out. Several brands of locally-produced **hot pepper sauce**, made from scotch bonnet peppers (small, bonnet-shaped, and very hot), onions, tomatoes, vinegar, and water, are always winners. The smooth, strong, locally-made **Tortuga Rum**, Cayman's number one export, is another favorite take-home item. So is **Tortuga Rum Cake**, a buttery, rich, and liquor-laden treat that enables you to get drunk and fat at the same time. Made from a century-old recipe, the cakes come in handsome tin containers that make good storage boxes when empty.

The other hot local item that many people find irresistible is **caymanite**, semi-precious dolomite stone thought to have been formed between 16 million and 25 million years ago. A beautiful stone found only in the Cayman Islands, it varies in color from beige to pink and brown, and when turned into pendants, rings, earrings, money clips, or key rings, makes a delightful memento or gift to take back home.

Although endangered and no longer farmed in the Cayman Islands, black coral, usually in the form of jewelry, is abundant in many stores. But buyers should beware; only jewelers licensed by the Caymanian government can sell it and unless your purchase comes with an official certificate it might be confiscated at Customs. Other items to be careful about are **turtle products** (shells, jewelry, oils, canned meat). Sold just about everywhere in the Cayman Islands, turtle products are not allowed into the US or several other countries.

While the largest concentration of stores is in downtown George Town, there are others in most busy tourist areas of Grand Cayman. Most stores in Cayman Brac and Little Cayman are tiny, and are usually in hotels.

Artifacts
Harbour Drive, George Town
Tel: 949 7477
A maritime and West Indian boutique specializing in antique maps, rare coins, coin jewelry, silver, enamel work, and antique scientific and marine instruments.

Blackbeard Liquors
Crewe Road, George Town
Tel: 949 8763
In addition to being a full-service liquor store, this is the home of Blackbeard's

Left: hats, baskets, and other items made of thatch palm are popular buys
Right: the famous Tortuga Rum Cake

Premium Rums, a locally produced rum that comes in 11 special flavors, including coconut, mango, peach, and banana.

Book Nook
Anchorage Centre, George Town
Tel: 949 7392
With two noisy pet parrots that greet customers, this cozy, friendly shop is jam-packed with books on the Cayman Islands, writing implements, coffee-table books, current novels and non-fiction, newspapers, magazines, and gifts. Occasionally it hosts readings by visiting authors.

British Outpost
Duty Free Centre, George Town
Tel: 949 0742
A large, exclusive store featuring top-quality gold chains, jewelry, black coral, sterling silver, gold coins, diamonds, key chains, cuff links, tie clips, and watches.

Cathy Church's Underwater Photo Gallery
Church Street, south of George Town
Tel: 949 7415
World-famous underwater photographer, Cathy Church, displays and sells her breathtaking shots of Cayman Islands' marine life and underwater topography.

Cayman Camera
South Church Street, George Town
Tel: 949 8359
A comprehensive array of regular and underwater cameras, loads of hi-tech photography equipment and all the necessary supplies, binoculars, and Cayman prints from local photographers.

Cayman Glassblowing Studio
North Church Street, George Town
Tel: 949 7020
Inspired by Cayman's vibrant marine life, artisan Stephen Zawistowski displays his unusual range of delicate glass sculptures here. He also stages interesting glass-blowing demonstrations. This branch is just a few minutes walk from the waterfront.

Ciara's Secret
Galeria Plaza, Seven Mile Beach
Tel: 945 5571
Tantalizing underwear and nightwear – lace lingerie, silk robes, pajamas, and luxurious satin nightgowns.

Coach Leather Factory Store
Anchorage Centre, George Town
Tel: 949 7477
Duty-free leather goods direct from the factory, including purses, wallets, briefcases, and backpacks.

De Watch Man
Duty Free Centre, George Town
Tel: 949 8964
The largest selection of duty-free watches in the Cayman Islands with real bargains on brand names such as Anne Klein, Nautica, Guess, and Storm of London.

Exotic Trading Post
Waterfront Centre, George Town
Tel: 949 3176
An interesting enclave of exotic treasures from around the world – European model boats, porcelain from Ecuador, stone fountains, Russian dolls, African masks, interesting West Indian wood-carvings, colorful Indonesian batik prints, embroidered tablecloths, bronze picture frames, clay jars, and hand-painted wooden room dividers. They will ship large items overseas for a fee.

Far Away Places
Shedden Road, George Town
Tel: 949 7477
A luxurious Irish linen shop with sheets, pillow cases, bedspreads, shams (bed throws), Battenberg lace, and crocheted tablecloths.

Above: no breakfast, but plenty of jewelry at Tiffany's

Grand Switzerland
Anchorage Shopping Centre, George Town
Tel: 946 2333
A fantastic assortment of Swiss watches, cultured pearls, black fresh-water pearls, tanzanite, sapphires, and emeralds.

Heritage Crafts and Gift Market
Harbour Drive, George Town
Tel: 945 6041
Classic Caribbean gifts such as straw hats, island music tapes and CDs, wood-carvings, shell jewelry, spices, teas, and coffee.

Island Casuals
Galeria Plaza, Seven Mile Beach
Tel: 945 0924
Elegant and casual wear – sundresses, sandals, shirts, swim suits, and straw hats.

Joe Tourist Caribbean Village
Paradise Road, George Town
Tel: 946 5638
Don't let the name turn you off. Part artists' retreat and part nature store, this unusual complex feels like an old Caymanian home with a thatched roof, sand floors, and tropical flowers. Owner Gilbert Nicoletta represents artists and craftsmen from all the islands and stocks calabash masks, thatch fans and bags.

Kennedy Gallery
West Shore Centre, West Bay
Tel: 949 8077
One of the finer galleries on the islands, Kennedy stocks an exclusive array of Wassi art – Jamaican-made pottery utilizing terracotta clay and a thin mineral glaze. The bowls, vases, plates, mugs, cups, and pitchers are all one-of-a-kind pieces with painted or etched tropical scenes in vibrant colors.

Kirk Jewelers
Cardinal Avenue, George Town
Tel: 949 7477
Diamonds, rubies, emeralds, and sapphires, and brand-name timepieces such as Rolex, Omega, Breitling Ebel, and Patek Philippe.

Little Darlings
Alexandra Place, George Town
Tel: 949 2580
Children's clothing in all sizes and price ranges, plus water-sports toys, dolls' houses, books, and art supplies.

Pure Art
South Church Street, George Town
Tel: 949 9133
This small but clever gallery housed in an old cottage is a treasure chest of goods from more than 200 local artists. Each room is packed with colorful arts and crafts, oil paintings, watercolors, hand-carved tableware, and whimsical thatch brooms made by Caymanian artist, Conrad Forbes.

Puro Rey Cigars
Seven Mile Beach
Tel: 945 4913
In addition to a large selection of hand-rolled Cuban cigars, this lavishly-stocked shop with a walk-in humidor has an impressive assortment of Jamaican, Nicaraguan, Honduran, Costa Rican, and Dominican cigars.

Tropical L'Attitude
Edward Street, George Town
Tel: 945 1233
A dazzling boutique filled with handcrafted gifts, hand-carved curio cabinets, batik bedspreads, hand-woven bags and baskets, and tropical-print beach wraps and sexy sarongs.

Tortuga Duty Free Liquors and Bakery
West Bay, near the Cayman Turtle Farm
Tel: 949 9247
A heady, sweet-smelling store and working bakery with an assortment of rum cakes, baked goods, souvenirs, bottled rums, rum creams, and rum liqueurs.

Venture Gallery
West Shore Centre, West Bay
Tel: 949 8657
Maritime artifacts from centuries of Cayman Islands' history, including gold coins, nautical antiques, silver, and maps.

Waterford & Wedgewood Gallery
Cardinal Avenue, George Town
Tel: 949 7477
An exquisite collection of Waterford crystal, including champagne flutes and wine glasses, and Wedgewood china plates, cups, and decorative plaques.

EATING OUT

Although spiked with a sassy West Indian attitude, Cayman Islands cuisine borrows from the heritage of all the ethnic groups that have settled on the islands during the past three centuries. Starting out with the earliest settlers, from England, Scotland, Wales, and Ireland, the islands forged a tradition of European cooking styles with an emphasis on stews, Cornish pasties, fried or cured fish, meats, and breads. The enslaved Africans brought their cultivation skills and the seeds of their homelands and added an interesting accent on vegetables and legumes (pulses). The Cayman tradition of 'jerking' meats and poultry (smoking them over burning pimento branches and wood) came from nearby Jamaica, as did the use of curry powder and Asian spices, brought to Jamaica by workers from the East Indies and China. A hint of Spanish and Portuguese spices and cooking styles also crept in, brought by mariners and settlers on Spanish-controlled islands.

As its foundation, Caymanian cuisine has always utilized the sea and incorporated the bounty of fish, turtles, crabs, conch, and lobsters that are easily found offshore. Herbs and spices often used in Caymanian cooking include garlic, thyme, nutmeg, allspice, and pimento. Local cakes and breads, usually heavy and dense, are commonly made from cassava, yam, corn, breadfruit, or sweet potato, and usually have a splash of coconut milk added for flavor.

A few typical dishes that really should be tried include conch, marinated in lime and served as a spicy stew, or fried as fritters; turtle, prepared as a steak, or in a stew

or soup; fish rundown, which means simmered in coconut milk with breadfruit or cassava; fish tea – a light clear soup; Johnny cakes – dense, fried breads; pumpkin soup; meat patties; fried plantains (bananas); coconut shrimp; red bean soup; rice and peas (not peas, in fact, but red kidney beans); jerk chicken or beef; sautéed *callaloo* (spinach-like greens); and freshly-squeezed papaya, mango, and guava juice.

Today, cuisine in the Cayman Islands is rich, sophisticated, and varied. There are over 300 restaurants on these three small islands, and along with native cooking, there are styles from around the world – Chinese, Thai, Japanese, Mexican, Indian, Italian, French, English, Spanish, Brazilian, Cuban, American, Middle Eastern, and African. Restaurant atmospheres range from casual seaside settings to elegant luxury, and fine wines from Europe, the United States, and South America are on most menus.

The following restaurant price guide is for the average cost of a full meal with a glass of wine or beer:

$ = under US$20
$$ = US$20–40
$$$ = above US$40

Grand Cayman

Café Mozart
West Bay Road
Seven Mile Beach
Tel: 946 2233
Authentic German and Austrian recipes in a cozy, Old World European setting. Some great dishes here include sautéed chicken livers, Hungarian goulash, pork medallions, beef stroganoff, tournedos Amadeus, wiener schnitzel, and gypsy schnitzel. $$$

Café Tabu
West Bay Road
Seven Mile Beach
Tel: 945 6333
A stylish and hip spot with a contemporary atmosphere and live jazz, Café Tabu offers an assortment of imaginative Asian dishes such as Malay lobster soup, curried garbanzo beans, *miso* duck broth, lemon grass coconut shrimp, wok-seared tuna, tandoori chicken, peas pilaf, glass noodle stir-fry, and sea bass in cilantro and lemon oil. $$$

Above: conch fritters are among the most typical, and delicious, of Cayman Island foods

Calypso Grill
Morgans Harbor
West Bay
Tel: 949 3948
Housed in a Caribbean cottage painted bright yellow, red, and purple, this seaside dining spot is full of West Indian character, with views of fishing boats coming in with their catch. A long mahogany bar offers cool cocktails and great wines, and some of the treats on the menu are pork paella, seafood paella, tuna *sashimi*, cracked conch, grilled shrimp, and *wahoo* seviche. $$$

Casa Havana
Inside the Westin Casuarina Resort
Seven Mile Beach
Tel: 945 3800
Heralded as the only AAA four-star restaurant in the Cayman Islands, this supremely elegant place received an award from *Wine Spectator* magazine and was deemed one of the best restaurants in the world for wine connoisseurs. The menu features classic Cuban dishes with a sophisticated flair, and tropical seafood specialties utilizing exotic fruits and vegetables. $$$

Coffee Grinder Gourmet Deli
West Bay Road
Seven Mile Beach
Tel: 949 4833
A classic deli with a gourmet twist in a casual setting offering large portions of cinnamon buns, bagels, smoked salmon platters, meat loaf, coleslaw, chicken noodle soup, and corned beef, roast beef, glazed ham, and turkey breast sandwiches. $

DJ's Cantina
Coconut Place
Seven Mile Beach
Tel: 945 4234
A lively and casual Mexican cantina with generous margaritas, and Mexican dishes such as shrimp tortillas, guacamole, burritos, and red-hot salsa. $$

Every Bloomin' Thing's Victorian Tea Room
South Church Street
George Town
Tel: 945 1701
A great escape from the hustle of downtown, this tranquil and soothing tea room in the eastern reaches of the capital is a popular hang-out for local people who come for the wide assortment of teas, coffees, and the delicious homemade scones, cakes, pies, soups, and sandwiches. $

Gateway to India
West Bay Road
Seven Mile Beach
Tel: 946 2815
Rich with an Indian decor of tapestries and artifacts, this recently-opened restaurant imports its spices directly from India, and includes specialty items such as shrimp Masala on a crispy rice *dosa*, vegetable samosas, mint coriander chutney, and an array of curry dishes. $$

Grand Old House
South Church Street
George Town
Tel: 949 9333
One of those places that must be seen, this enduring restaurant in a stately Caribbean Great House (dating back to 1908) is a local legend that is often used for island weddings and lavish balls. Before coming to Grand Cayman, resident chef Kandathil Mathai cooked for royalty and politicians such as Prince Charles, Margaret Thatcher, and US President Ronald Reagan. Featuring European and New World cuisine in dishes such as tenderloin black Angus beef, potato-crusted tuna, lobster sauteed with shallots, and baby lamb, it also has impeccable service and an extensive wine list. Reservations recommended. $$$

Left: there is no shortage of places to enjoy a casual lunch

Heritage Kitchen
Behind Powell's Heritage Museum
West Bay
Tel: 949 3477
An authentic Caribbean seaside shack, with picnic tables and benches, run by a great Jamaican cook who serves curried chicken, fried fish, conch fritters, fish tea, and a melange of local vegetables. $

Kaibo Yacht Club & Restaurant
Water Cay Road
Rum Point
Tel: 947 9975
Overlooking the sleepy shores of Kaibo Beach, this elegant dining spot has an eclectic blend of Caribbean and New Orleans cuisine. From classic Caymanian fish dishes to spicy seafood *gumbos*, crawfish stew, and *jambalaya*. Reservations suggested. $$$

Lantana's Restaurant & Bar
West Bay Road
Seven Mile Beach
Tel: 945 5595
Offering contemporary Caribbean and Cuban cuisine with an international flair, this relaxing place features fresh snapper, shrimp, scallops, grouper, tuna, black bean soup, pork tenderloin, and rack of lamb, with coconut parfaits and Cayman lime pie for dessert. $$

Liberty Restaurant
Rev. Blackman Road
West Bay
Tel: 949 3226
For 20 years, the comfortable Liberty has been catering to families, with seafood specialties and a children's menu that includes burgers and fries, chicken fingers, turtle stew, curried goat, and lemon meringue pie. $$

Mount Fuji Sushi
West Bay Polo Club
Seven Mile Beach
Tel: 949 9892
An authentic sushi and sake bar with a Japanese chef; *miso* soup, *tempura* and *teriyaki* dishes, and every form of sushi. $$

Portofino Wreck View
Colliers Road
East End
Tel: 947 2700
Catering to a mix of local people and tourists, this fine Italian eatery is known for its great service and traditional Italian dishes: veal *scaloppini*, lasagna, seafood pasta, antipasto, and garlic bread. $$

Ristorante Pappagallo
Conch Point Road
West Bay
Tel: 949 1119
With a thatch-palm roof and a wooden bridge meandering over a secluded lagoon, this spot is constructed out of bamboo, local stones, and marble. Surrounding the property is a 14-acre (5.5-ha) bird sanctuary, and inside are dozens of caged, exotic macaws, cockatoos, and African gray parrots. The menu features Northern Italian cuisine with homemade pastas, garlic *foccacia* bread, seafood dishes, and dessert pastries. $$$

Thai Orchid
Queens Court
Seven Mile Beach
Tel: 949 7955
In a small shopping center, this classic Thai eatery has Bangkok chefs who whip up exotic dishes such as Thai *satey*, bean thread noodle soup, *phad* Thai, crispy duck in ginger sauce, vegetable curry, and sauteed shrimp with bamboo shoots. $$

Left: local in a beach-side café

The Edge Café
Bodden Town
Tel: 947 2140
Run by Caymanian Hartwell Wood, and Philippe Gros, a Frenchman, this romantic seaside spot with great sunset views offers a menu that combines the best of French and Caymanian cuisine, with dishes such as blackened *mahi-mahi* with tomato and basil sauce and jumbo shrimp in a Pernod cream sauce. Reservations are strongly recommended. $$

The Links Restaurant
Safe Haven
Seven Mile Beach
Tel: 949 5988
One of the finest gourmet restaurants in Grand Cayman, The Links features a sophisticated fusion cuisine menu, a well-rounded wine list, and a stunning view of the North Sound. $$$

Tree House
North Church Street
George Town
Tel: 945 0155
Nestled among the trees on a sandy cove with sweeping views of the George Town harbor, this island-style restaurant has a varied Greek and European menu with dishes such as spinach and feta cheese dip, a variety of Spanish *tapas*, chicken *souvlaki*, delicious grilled seafood kebabs, and fresh-baked pitta bread. $

Cayman Brac

Almond Tree Café
Mac Plaza
Spot Bay
Tel: 948 0372
Owner Julie Ann McLaughlin does the home-style cooking in this small and friendly place and serves heaped portions for lunch and dinner that include oxtail soup, fried fish, curried chicken, beef stew, saltfish and *ackee*, pepper steak, and meat patties – unmissable delicious Caribbean flavors. Warm, charming, and delightful to talk to, Miss McLaughlin on occasion even catches the fish herself. The cafe also has American staples burgers and hot dogs for the less adventurous visitor. $

Aunt Sha's Kitchen
Dennis Point
South Side
Tel: 948 1587
Open seven days a week, this indoor/outdoor restaurant doubles as a late-night pool hall, and features a combination Caymanian/Chinese menu that includes sweet and sour chicken, chop suey, grilled lobster, fried fish, and lemon pie. $

Captain's Table
West End
near Brac Caribbean Beach Resort
Tel: 948 1418
An, elegant, air-conditioned restaurant with candlelight and linen tablecloths, Captain's Table has a broad menu that includes steaks, burgers, chicken, and several seafood pasta dishes. $$

G & M Diner
West End
near Tibbetts Square
Tel: 948 1272
A casual, family-style diner that serves both American and Caymanian-style breakfasts, lunches, and dinners. $

Little Cayman

Hungry Iguana
Iguana Court, near Paradise Villas
Tel: 948 0007
Named for an iguana known to roam nearby, this large, modern, seaside eatery features breakfast buffets, and lunches and dinners that include fish sandwiches, burgers, salads, steaks, and prime rib. $

Southern Cross Club
South Hole Sound
Tel: 948 1099
The restaurant, in Southern Cross Club dive resort, is a pleasant spot featuring gourmet Caymanian and American-style dishes. $$$

Valda's Kitchen
Near the airport
No phone
A casual, local eatery run by Miss Valda herself, that serves Caymanian specialties such as stewed fish, rice and peas, and, of course, conch fritters. $

NIGHTLIFE

Evenings in the Cayman Islands begin with a wonderful piece of free entertainment – the local phenomenon known as the green flash, a natural ray of green light that dances briefly on the horizon as the sun gently slips into the Caribbean Sea.

When darkness sets in, the nights are marked by reggae, wafting from seaside bars, lively steel-band performances, and dancing under the stars. Also on hand, on Grand Cayman, are comedy clubs, community theater acts, dance troupes, discos, and dinner cruises.

In Cayman Brac and Little Cayman, the majority of evening entertainment is staged by the hotels, and consists mostly of hotel-hosted beach barbecues, dance parties, and casual after-diving cocktails by the pool.

The legal drinking age is 18, and this is taken seriously – identification is often checked at the door. There are, of course, laws governing drinking and driving, and these, as well as plain common sense, mean that taxi services are recommended for all premeditated bacchanalia.

As required by local law, all bars and nightclubs close at 1am on weekdays and at midnight on Saturday and Sunday. Although many bars are open, there is no live music or entertainment on Sunday. A local entertainments' guide called *What's Hot Cayman*, offers current news about nightlife on the island and is available free at most hotels.

Although evening entertainment shuts down early there is still lots of fun to be had on the Cayman Islands. Whether you want to have a quiet drink, or dance your socks off, it's all here.

Bars/Nightclubs

Bed
Island Complex
Seven Mile Beach
Tel: 949 7199
A funky enclave that caters to an upscale clientele, Bed hosts well-known DJs from New York, London, Spain, and South Africa who spin a creative melange of pop, jazz, Latin, reggae, and R&B tunes.

Blue Parrot Bar and Café
Church Street
George Town
Tel: 949 9094
With a resident macaw as a mascot, this spot is a favorite watering hole of local people who come for the inexpensive drinks and cool sea breezes.

Captain Bryan's Patio Bar
North Church Street
George Town
Tel: 949 6163
Heralding itself as the 'best British pub for 5,000 miles,' Captain Bryan's has been a favorite with the ex-pat community for many years. The pub offers an extensive selection of beers and gin, hosts darts tournaments, and wild jam sessions.

Club Inferno
West Bay
Hell
Tel: 949 3263
What else would a club in Hell be called? Live Caribbean, Latin, and country music with a down-home local atmosphere, right next door to the Hell Post Office.

Fidel Murphy's
West Bay Road
Seven Mile Beach
Tel: 949 5189
Although it's hard to imagine such a thing, an 'Irish' Fidel Castro is the theme of this lively saloon that features tall drinks, Cuban cigars, and live music on weekends.

Hard Rock Café
Church Street
George Town
Tel: 945 2020
Starting off with a bustling singles scene at happy hour, this world-renowned chain, known for its music memorabilia and potent drinks, continues to party well into the night, and has a Caribbean island theme that includes an old acoustic guitar once owned by singer Jimmy Buffett.

Hyatt Regency Caribbean Night
West Bay Road
Seven Mile Beach
Tel: 949 1234
A regular, island-style outdoor party held at the Hyatt Regency Grand Cayman pool, with fire eaters, limbo dancers, steel pan performers, plenty of rum, and a buffet of Caribbean specialties.

Legendz
Falls Shopping Centre
George Town
Tel: 945 1950
Vibrant, lively and loud, this nightclub is popular with the young crowd.

Loggia Lounge
Hyatt Regency Resort
Seven Mile Beach
Tel: 949 1234
A sophisticated piano bar that attracts a classy crowd of discerning Caymanians and

tourists, who come to sip martinis, nibble on conch fritters, and puff on expensive Cuban cigars.

Lone Star Bar & Grill
West Bay Road
Seven Mile Beach
Tel: 945 5175
Rated one of the 'top 100 bars in the world' by *Newsweek* magazine, this American-style sports-theme saloon attracts beer-drinking dive masters, bourbon-drinking bankers, and a slew of tourists drinking all kinds of things, who all mingle as one.

Ports of Call Bar
West Bay Road
George Town,
Tel: 949 7729
Tucked inside the Wharf Restaurant complex, the Ports of Call is a romantic, waterfront hideaway that is very popular with couples. Its nightly live music ranges from Paraguayan harpists to slow-moving dance tunes.

Royal Palms Beach Club
Seven Mile Beach
Tel: 945 6358
On the former site of the old Royal Palms Hotel, this open-air, thatch-palm-roofed beach bar has a relaxed and casual atmosphere, and features live island-style music Wednesday through Saturday nights.

Left: eating outdoors on a balmy evening is one of the joys of the Cayman Islands
Above: beginning an evening at the Cayman Kai Resort.

Rum Point Bar & Restaurant
Rum Point
Grand Cayman
Tel: 947 9412
These days, this is where George Novak, the legendary 'barefoot man' of Grand Cayman, plays on a few nights a week. About 20 years ago, Novak sang his original songs barefoot in the sand on Seven Mile Beach and now he's a local tradition. A blend of calypso, reggae, soca, and country, his act is worth seeking out.

Sharkey's Nightclub
Cayman Falls Shopping Centre
Seven Mile Beach
Tel: 945 5366
Live rock bands blast their tunes here as the dance floor pulsates with action. There are also big-screen music theme nights and comedy acts.

The Next Level Nightclub and Lounge
West Bay Road
Seven Mile Beach
Tel: 949 7169
A strobe lights and glittering disco ball kind of place that has a jam-packed dance floor on weekends. With some of the best DJs on Grand Cayman spinning the discs, the entertainment here ranges from American rock and hip-hop to trendy techno and Euro-style dance nights.

West Bay Polo Club and Bar
West Bay Road
Seven Mile Beach
Tel: 949 9892
A boisterous but friendly sports bar complete with 15 large-screen televisions that broadcast major football, soccer, basketball, baseball, cricket, boxing, and tennis events from around the world.

Dance/Choral/Theater

Cayman Islands National Dance Company
Savannah
Grand Cayman
Tel: 949 9444
Also known as Dance Unlimited, this local troupe of 20 dancers founded in 1988 by Jamaica School of Dance graduate, Lorna Reid, offers a week-long spring season (the month varies each year) and a two-day Christmas show. Held at both the Harquail Theatre and the Prospect Playhouse, the performances are a diverse array of African, West Indian, modern, and ballet styles.

Cayman National Choir
Grand Cayman
Tel: 949 7800
Local musicians, along with visiting US musicians, perform with this company during a Spring Music Festival in May, and a classic Christmas production in December at various locations on Grand Cayman.

Above: what could be nicer than a dinner cruise on the Jolley Roger as the sun sets over the islands? **Right**: Stingray beer, the islands local brew

Harquail Theatre
West Bay Road
Seven Mile Beach
Tel: 949 5054
Managed by the Cayman Drama Society, this small theater stages five major productions each year. They include works created by Caymanian and West Indian playwrights and range from comedies to dramas and musicals. It also offers intimate dinner and theater shows on Friday nights.

Prospect Playhouse
Red Bay
Grand Cayman
Tel: 949 5477
A 330-seat community theater that hosts local drama, comedy, and musical productions, visiting stage shows, art exhibits, and theatrical workshops.

Dinner Cruises
Jolley Roger Dinner Cruise
Bayside Dock
George Town
Tel: 945 7245
This replica of a 17th-century galleon sets sail most evenings at dusk for a romantic dinner cruise that is very popular among honeymooners and young couples. Along with a glorious sunset and the peaceful ride, the cruise includes rum punch, and a full dinner with wine.

Red Sail Sunset Cruises
Seven Mile Beach
Tel: 945 5965
Operating from both Seven Mile Beach and Rum Point, Red Sail runs two-hour sunset sails with cocktails and appetizers, and dinner cruises with three-course meals.

Comedy Clubs
Chuckles Comedy Club
Tel: 945 5077
With shows that cater to the tastes of both local residents and tourists, this clever troupe performs at several clubs and hotels on Grand Cayman.

Coconuts Comedy Club
Tel: 949 6887
A hilarious local troupe that performs at various venues on Grand Cayman, including Legendz Nightclub in George Town *(see page 75)*.

Cinema
Cinema I & II
West Bay Road
George Town
Tel: 949 4011
Although there are numerous video rental stores throughout the Cayman Islands, there is only one movie theater – and this is it. With a double-screen, it offers current American films Monday through Saturday nights.

Above: live music in the bars and clubs

CALENDAR OF EVENTS

Scattered throughout the year, several vibrant festivals take place in the Cayman Islands. Mostly held outdoors, they are joyous, colorful spectacles, many of which pay tribute to the islands' maritime and cultural heritage. The following is a brief list.

February

mid-February: a kaleidoscope of vivid purple and pink sets the mood at the Queen Elizabeth II Botanic Park, when it pays tribute to the tropical glory of the island with the annual **Orchid Show**. With heady scents filling the air, there are orchid displays, horticultural lectures and discussions, orchid-growing demonstrations, and exotic plants for sale. Tel: 947 9462.

late February: the pre-Lenten frenzy of the **Mardi Gras** festival stirs up the tiny island of Little Cayman and the entire community takes part in the festivities. As the 40 days of Lent are tied to Easter, the exact date varies from year to year. Along with naming a king and queen, the annual island-style jump-up includes elaborate float parades, costume contests (some of the costumes are quite extraordinary), street dances, live music, fireworks over the water, and, of course, plenty of rum. Tel: 948 1010.

March/April

early March: the **Cayman Islands National Trust Gala** is an elegant, black-tie affair in George Town with gourmet foods, fine wines and live music. The gala's mission is to raise funds for the preservation of the island's natural environment as well as places of historic significance. Tel: 949 0121.

mid-March: the culture and arts extravaganza known as **Cayfest** envelopes the island of Grand Cayman for several days and means plenty of live music, drama, dance, and arts and crafts displays. There are also special children's activities, fun-packed festival days, boat launches and regattas, and a real party atmosphere, with local food and drink on sale. Tel: 949 5457.

In conjunction with the Grand Cayman event, Cayman Brac hosts its own **Cayfest Seaside Regatta** with both sailing and power boats taking part.

March 17: the **St Patrick's Day Jog** on Grand Cayman was inaugurated by Caymanian descendants of Irish settlers. Beginning and ending at the Britannia Golf Course (Tel: 949 8020), the 5K-run (3 miles/ 5 km) awards several prizes to both winners and losers.

mid- to late March: the waters off Grand Cayman come alive with the **Round the Island Regatta**. Organised by the Cayman Islands Sailing Club, it is one of the more competitive races in the Caribbean. This four-day race and on-shore party includes crafts ranging from small dinghies to sleek 80-ft (24-m) catamarans. Tel: 947 7913.

late March to mid-April: an annual **Easter Bash** is held in Little Cayman that includes food and festivities and an auction of arts and crafts to benefit the Little Cayman National Trust.

May/June

early May: the **Cayman Islands International Fishing Tournament** attracts keen anglers from all over the world to compete in several categories. Along with cash prizes and trophies, participating fishermen and women always go home with tall tales of big fish, which are often as enjoyable in the re-telling as they were at the time.

throughout May: for those who look to the green for fun, a couple of the golf tournaments on the May docket include the annual **Cayman Islands Chamber of Commerce Golf Classic**, and the **Cinco de Mayo Corona Golf Tournament** at the Links.

Above: island flowers: the annual National Trust Gala raises money for the preservation of flora and fauna as well as places of historic interest

late May: the yearly **Batabano Carnival** (pronounced *bata-banoo*) comes to downtown George Town. Featuring classic carnival music and live calypso and soca bands, the annual jubilee is also noted for its array of concession stands offering tasty tidbits of Caymanian and Caribbean cuisine, a large float parade, plenty of costumed merrymakers, and stop-all-the-traffic street dances. There is an attractive prize for the best costume in the parade, but only outfits made in the Cayman Islands are eligible for the competition.

mid-June: **Aviation Week** in all three islands. This means fly-in caravans from all over North America, daring air shows, live music, and aviation-oriented displays and seminars.

July

early July: island-style cuisine is the theme of the popular annual fete known as the **Taste of Cayman**, hosted by the local restaurant association. Turtle stew, Caymanian fish, conch fritters, and conch chowders are among the many treats to be tasted, as well as the ubiquitous, rich and potent rum cake. Tel: 949 8522.

mid-July: the hard-fought **Governor's Cup** sailing challenge takes place. The waters around Grand Cayman are jam-packed with sophisticated racing teams from all over the world as well as local favorites, as fans cheer them on from the beaches and bars.

September/October

mid-September: **Cayman Madness Dive Vacation** lures divers from around the world for a week of underwater treasure hunts, beach parties, live concerts, and prizes.

late October: Blackbeard and his buccaneers come to town during swashbuckling **Pirates' Week Festival**, when all three islands take part in the rousing revelry.

Without a doubt the grandest event in the Cayman Islands, this yearly bash includes a mock invasion of the George Town harbor, complete with costumed pirates. Also part of the program are an underwater treasure hunt, children's games and rides, jazz and reggae concerts, food fairs, cultural heritage displays, golf tournaments, teen disco parties, dance and costume contests, a 5K-

run (3 miles/5 km), and firework displays. It's all in honor of the Cayman Islands' maritime heritage. Events can actually run for upto 10 days.

November

early November: Seven Mile Beach is the location of the **Annual Turtle Release**, when hundreds of turtles from the Cayman Turtle Farm are released back to the wild. The green sea turtles, an endangered species, are born and reared on the farm in Grand Cayman as part of a breed-and-release program. So far more than 30,000 turtles have been returned to the Caribbean Sea and divers regularly report sightings of the creatures. Visitors and local people turn out to witness the event. Tel: 949 3894

December

The Christmas spirit sets the tone for December, of course, and traditional holiday celebrations fill the air throughout the month. Home-owners on all the Cayman islands compete in the annual **Christmas House Lighting Contest** and the result is spectacular display of twinkling lights, illuminated Santas, and even a few reindeer complete with sunglasses. There are also seasonal evenings of carol singing on the steps of the George Town Courthouse, tree-lighting ceremonies, and a Santa Claus Landing Party for the children.

Right: pirates on parade in the October Pirates' Week Festival

Practical
Information

GETTING THERE

By Air

Several airlines offer regularly scheduled flights to Grand Cayman from the US, Great Britain, Jamaica, Honduras, and Cuba. From Miami, there are more than 45 direct flights a week to Grand Cayman and the flight time is 1 hour and 20 minutes. Grand Cayman's Owen Roberts International Airport (tel: 949 7733), which receives over 100 flights per week, is a modern facility with fast and efficient service that includes a helpful tourist information desk.

Cayman Airways and Island Air offer flights from Grand Cayman to Cayman Brac with a flight time of about 40 minutes. Aside from charter services, the only airline that regularly flies to Little Cayman is Island Air, with flights departing from both Grand Cayman and Cayman Brac.

When departing the Cayman Islands, visitors are required to pay a departure tax of US$12.50 per person and to check in for their flights at least 1½ hours prior to departure. No departure taxes are charged for inter-island travel within the Cayman Islands.

By Sea

Although it's a major cruise destination, the Cayman Islands guards against congestion and overcrowding by allowing no more than four large cruise ships to sail into port at any one time. Several companies regularly sail to Grand Cayman, including: Carnival, Celebrity, Commodore, Costa, Cunard, Dolphin, Holland America, Norwegian, Princess, Royal Caribbean, and Sun Line. Most of these companies begin their tours in Miami, Fort Lauderdale, or San Juan. For several years, no cruise ships were allowed into port on Sunday, but that ban has now been lifted.

Ships are required to anchor offshore and use tenders to ferry their passengers to either the North or the South Dock Terminals in

George Town. Situated fairly close together, both terminals are within easy walking distance of the many restaurants, visitor attractions, and shopping centers in downtown George Town.

The Cayman Islands is also an extremely popular port of call for privately-owned sailboats and yachts, and many marinas throughout the islands offer moorings for rent by the day or the week. There is no ferry service that connects the three Cayman Islands by sea.

TRAVEL ESSENTIALS

When to Visit

The most popular time to visit the Cayman Islands is from mid-December through mid-April. It is also the most expensive when it comes to hotel rates. Fleeing the cold winter, northerners from the US, the UK and Canada flock to the islands for warmth and sunshine. This is also the busiest time of year for cruise ships in the Caribbean.

The summer season of July and August means family vacation time for many, so these months bring a boost in visitor arrivals. And in the past few years, the Cayman Islands has promoted itself as a spring-break destination, when college students from across the US descend upon Grand Cayman.

Left: a cruise ship dwarfs a traditional-style galleon
Above Right: the Angel of the Ocean keeps watch over the port

The 'shoulder' seasons of spring and fall are the quietest and least expensive times of all. The one exception, however, is during the late October Pirates' Week Festival when all three islands are packed with tourists, and hotel rooms are booked many months in advance.

GETTING ACQUAINTED

Geography

Situated about 20 degrees north of the equator in the crystal-clear Caribbean Sea, the three coral atoll islands that make up the Cayman Islands are 150 miles (242 km) south of Cuba, 480 miles (772 km) south of Miami, and 180 miles (290 km) northwest of Jamaica. Although visitors often refer to them as 'the Caymans,' locals never do; they always call their home the Cayman Islands.

The largest and most developed is Grand Cayman (population 38,000; pronounced *kaymón*) at 22 miles (35 km) long and 4 miles (6.5 km) wide. Cayman Brac (population 1,600) is 12 miles (19 km) long by a little over 1 mile (1.6 km) wide. And Little Cayman (population 120) is 10 miles (16 km) long and 1 mile (1.6 km) wide.

Except for the bluff on Cayman Brac that rises to 140 ft (43 m), the islands are relatively flat, with no mountains or rivers. Their interiors are solid limestone and mostly covered in dense woodlands. Beneath the sea, however, the terrain is a dramatic expanse of submarine mountain outcrops.

Between the Cayman Islands and nearby Jamaica is the Cayman Trough, also called the Cayman Trench, with the deepest point (25,000 ft/7,620 m) in the Caribbean Sea.

Population

The native-born people who live in the Cayman Islands are called Caymanians. One-third of the population is foreign-born (mostly American, British, and Jamaican citizens), and over 100 nationalities are present. The majority of Caymanians, however, are multiracial descendants of early English, Irish, Scottish, Welsh, and African settlers. Because the islands were never a major slave colony, and because many foreigners came here as seafarers, there is a great deal of ethnic and racial tolerance among the residents.

Government and Economy

The Cayman Islands is a British Overseas Territory led by a governor, an appointee of the Queen. The governor leads the Executive Council, which includes three official and five elected ministers. Offshore finance and tourism are the mainstays of the local economy, providing local people with the highest standard of living in the Caribbean.

Religion/How Not to Offend

In general, Caymanians are conservative, respectful and religious people. There is a slight formality in the way they interact with each other; people are introduced as Mr, Mrs or Miss, and manners are always of the utmost importance.

Above: inter-island flights utilize small, propeller-powered planes

There are over 75 churches listed in the phone book, and Sunday is a time devoted to prayer and family. Over 90 percent of the local population are Christian, with the Anglican Church and Seventh-Day Adventists being the most common denominations.

There are no nudist beaches; public nudity and topless bathing are prohibited by law.

Language

The official language of the Cayman Islands is English. The Caymanian accent is delightful to the ear, and includes intonations from Scottish, Irish, Welsh, and Cornish accents.

Visas and Passports

All visitors to the Cayman Islands (including cruise-ship passengers) are required to possess a current passport as well as a return plane ticket. US, Canadian, and most European citizens can enter the Cayman Islands without a visa and are allowed to stay for up to six months. People of other nationalities need to check with their own governments for current requirements.

Upon arrival, immigration forms that include information about where you will be staying in the islands, must be completed. A copy of the form is stamped by officials and the traveler must keep it until leaving the Cayman Islands.

Work permit requirements are very strict, and require a great deal of government paperwork in advance. In George Town, the immigration office can be found at the Government Administration Building on Elgin Avenue.

Vaccinations

No vaccinations are required.

Customs

Upon arrival, all visitors must pass through customs and declare all items of value, such as cameras and jewelry. The duty-free allowance when entering the Cayman Islands is approximately 2 pints (1 liter) of liquor or 7 pints (4 liters) of wine, and 200 cigarettes or 50 cigars. Plants, flowers, fruits, vegetables, and many food products are not allowed into the islands.

The possession of illegal drugs can lead to imprisonment as well as fines, and suitcases are opened and searched at the airport on occasion. The possession of firearms is also illegal.

Upon departure, US citizens are allowed to return home with up to US$400-worth of purchases without paying duty. Turtle products such as shells or canned meat cannot be taken into the US or through the US while in transit to other countries.

Weather

The Cayman Islands has a tropical climate that varies only slightly throughout the year. The average temperature range is 78–92ºF (25–33ºC) in summer and 68–82ºF (20–28ºC) in winter. Annual rainfall averages about 68 inches (173 cm) a year. The islands are usually cooled off in the afternoon by showers during the rainy season (May through October), and in winter delightful sea breezes are constant. Trade winds, usually blowing from the east, are prevalent.

The hurricane season runs from June through November, and a major storm can wreak havoc on a vacation. The islands are well prepared, however, and modern hotels have been built to withstand winds of severe magnitude. In case of a serious threat, an evacuation plan goes into effect, and tourists are asked to leave the island. Storms are monitored regularly, with updates reported on local radio and television stations, especially during a hurricane 'watch' or 'warning' period. The Cayman Islands Hurricane Hotline can be reached on all three islands by calling tel: 946 3333.

The temperature of the sea remains warm (75–85ºF/24–29ºC) throughout most of the year except for a month or two in winter. Surface waves are usually larger and more powerful on the windward side of the islands.

Clothing

With a year-round tropical climate, casual summer clothing is always worn in the Cayman Islands. Even in the capital, George Town, it is rare to see a man wearing a formal suit and tie. Except for a few of the finer restaurants, where jackets for men are suggested, a crisp, collared shirt is all that is expected.

Shorts, tank tops, and sandals are commonly worn by both men and women.

Bathing costumes, however, are unacceptable in commercial establishments and should be reserved for beaches, boats, and resort areas.

Sun hats or visors are a must, especially in the summer months, and sunglasses are suggested. Umbrellas are rarely needed, except for protection from the sun. The beach sand can get very hot so sandals are a good idea. Smart, resort-casual is the best way to describe the dress in most nightclubs and better restaurants. A sweater, light jacket, or shawl for evenings is suggested for women, since many establishments run their air-conditioning full blast.

Electricity
Throughout the Cayman Islands, the current is 120 volts and standard US flat pin plugs are used. Electrical appliances made in the US do not need adapters, but most European-made ones do. Power cuts are rare.

Time Zone
All three Cayman Islands operate on Eastern Standard Time which is the same as the time in New York and five hours behind Greenwich Mean Time. They do not adopt daylight savings time, so between April and October they are one hour behind EST.

MONEY MATTERS

Currency
The official currency of the Cayman Islands is the Cayman Island dollar, usually fixed at a rate of about CI$1.00 per US$1.20. Currency bills are issued in units of $100, $50, $25, $10, $5, and $1. US dollars are accepted everywhere in the islands so Americans need not change their currency.

Banking/Cash Machines/Currency Exchange
There are over 500 banks licensed in the Cayman Islands. Most are open Mon–Fri, 9am–4pm, except on Little Cayman where the one bank is only open on Wednesday. They all offer a fixed rate of exchange that rarely varies. Most large hotels also offer exchange services. There is no black market. Cash machines (ATMs) are abundant and are located at banks, grocery stores, and shopping centers throughout the three islands.

Credit Cards
While a few small vendors will only take cash, the majority of businesses accept credit cards. Most establishments post a list of the cards they will accept; this usually includes MasterCard, Visa, American Express, Diners Club, and Discover.

Tipping
Tipping at the rate of 15 percent is common in most restaurants and some include the gratuity on the bill, so check before adding it. Although tips to taxi drivers, baggage handlers and maids are welcome, locals in general are not at all demanding when it comes to tips. Bell hops and airport baggage handlers customarily get $1 to $2 per bag.

Departure Tax
Some airlines add the price of the Cayman Islands government departure tax to the price of the ticket. If not, a fee of US$12.50 is collected at the airport. This fee is included in the price of most cruises.

GETTING AROUND

Rental Cars
The Cayman Islands are easy to get around and driving is simple and safe. Except for George Town and the Seven Mile Beach area of Grand Cayman, there is very little traffic. Driving is on the left and most rental cars have automatic transmissions. Rates are very reasonable and the service is hassle-free. The purchase of a local driving permit is required by law and costs US$12. Cars, jeeps, and vans are all available. Drivers must be at least 18, have a valid driver's license, and a credit card.

Among the car rental firms are:
Grand Cayman: Andy's (tel: 949 8111), Budget (tel: 949 5605), Cico (tel: 949 2468), Coconut (tel: 949 4377), Economy (tel: 949

Above: Caymanian heraldic symbol

9550 or 949 8992),Hertz (tel: 949 2280), and Soto's (tel: 945 2424).

Cayman Brac: Brac Rent-a-Car (tel: 948 1515), B & S Motors (tel: 948 1646), Four Ds (tel: 948 0459).

Little Cayman: McLaughlin (tel: 948 1000).

Taxis

Taxis in Grand Cayman are not metered. There are fixed fares from the airport to various locations, with extra charges for large pieces of luggage and more than four passengers. Taxis can also be hired for local transportation and guided tours. A minimum fee of CI$4 for the first mile (1.6 km) is the rule. Taxis can be found at the airport, major hotels, and most public places around Grand Cayman. A few useful numbers are:

Grand Cayman: Ace (tel: 949 3576), Cayman Cab (tel: 947 1173), Holiday (tel: 945 4491), Webster's (tel: 947 1718).

Cayman Brac: Elo Estaban (tel: 948 0220), Maple Edwards (tel: 948 0395).

Little Cayman: Most hotels on the islands provide local transportation.

Public Transportation

A regular public bus system finally came to Grand Cayman in 1998 and now works quite well. The main terminal is near the Public Library on Edward Street in George Town and there are eight routes around the island that go to West Bay, Bodden Town, East End, and North Side. One-way fares are about CI$2, and the buses operate daily from 6am to 11pm. For information, tel: 945 5100.

Ferry

There is no ferry service connecting the three islands but the reliable and fun Rum Pointer Ferry, a 120-passenger vessel, runs back and forth to Rum Point from Grand Cayman's Hyatt Regency Hotel (tel: 949 9098) several times a day. The cost is US$15 for the round-trip and reservations are suggested.

Tour Operators

Several companies offer regular day-trip tours and specially designed tours.

Grand Cayman: Majestic Tours, tel: 949 7773, Reality Tours, tel: 947 7200, Reid's Premier Tours, tel: 945 3345.

Cayman Brac: D&M Tours, tel: 948 2307.

HOURS AND HOLIDAYS

Business Hours

Stores and businesses are usually open Mon–Sat, 9am–5pm, and they do not close for siestas. Nearly all forms of commerce shut down on Sunday, including grocery stores, markets, and tourist gift shops.

Public Holidays

New Year's Day (1 January)
Ash Wednesday (date variable, depending on Easter)
Good Friday (date variable)
Easter Monday (date variable)
Discovery Day (third Monday in May)
Queen's Birthday (mid-June)
Constitution Day (first Monday in July)
Remembrance Day (second or third Monday in November)
Christmas Day (25 December)
Boxing Day (26 December)

ACCOMMODATION

Tourism is the backbone of the local economy, and the Cayman Islands are noted for modern accommodations, including over 5,000 'tourist rooms' that range from luxury hotels and condos to small inns and dive resorts. Because it caters to the mid- and upscale markets, bargain hotels are hard to find, but they do exist. Overall, the quality of service in most properties is excellent.

The government publishes an annual hotel rates and facts guide, obtainable from the tourist board. There are also two helpful websites, www.caymanresorts.com and www.caymanvillas.com. A government 'bed tax' of 10 percent is added to all hotel bills, and many properties also add a 10 percent service/gratuity charge as well.

Right: there are quite a few stylish old American cars on the islands

Prices vary according to the time of year, with winter months costing on average 40 percent more than summer. Rates for the hotels listed below are in US dollars and are based on a nightly, double-occupancy stay.

$$$$ = over $300
$$$ = between $200 and $300
$$ = between $100 and $200
$ = under $100

Grand Cayman
Beachcomber Condominiums
Seven Mile Beach
Tel: 945 4470
www.beachcomber1.com
Located in the center of Seven Mile Beach, this 24-unit, luxury condo has elegant two- and three-bedroom apartments. Ocean-side pool and water-sports. $$$$

Britannia Villas
Seven Mile Beach/Britannia Golf Course
Tel: 949 1234 or 800 233 1234
www.britanniavillas.com
Two- and three-bedroom units with elegant British colonial architecture and decor, fully equipped kitchens, and all amenities. Guests have access to the Hyatt Regency resort golf, pools, and 24-hour room service. $$$$

Grand Cayman Marriott Beach Resort
West Bay Road
Tel: 949 0088 or 800 228 9290
www.marriott.com
Right on Seven Mile Beach, this lush state-of-the-art chain resort has lagoons, water-falls, exotic flora, and stunning ocean views. The 300 guest rooms are luxurious; on-site amenities include a gym, Jacuzzi, tennis courts, water-sports, dive shop, and several restaurants. $$$$

Hyatt Regency Grand Cayman Resort
Seven Mile Beach
Tel: 949 1234
www.hyatt.com
A sprawling, luxurious resort with every amenity, this is a destination in itself. With a country club atmosphere, it includes plush beach-front villas and suites, a full-service spa, gym, tennis, children's activities, restaurants, bars, water-sports, and golf. $$$$

Rum Run Villa
Cayman Kai
Tel: 945 4144
A pretty, two-bedroom villa on the beach, within walking distance of restaurants, tennis, and water-sports. $$$

Spanish Reef Resort
West Bay
Tel: 949 3765 or 800 482 3483
An all-inclusive resort with a casual, tropical atmosphere, beautiful, palm-lined beach and a coral reef within swimming distance. It also has a freshwater pool, Jacuzzi, restaurant, bar, and scuba diving instructors on staff. All meals and use of a vehicle are included in the room rate. $$$

The Retreat Condominiums at Rum Point
Rum Point
Tel: 947 9135
Luxurious condos on the beach overlooking North Sound in the quiet Rum Point area of Grand Cayman, with fully-equipped kitchens, screened terraces, tennis courts, racquet-ball court, pool, fishing, and scuba diving services. $$$

Coconut Harbour Hotel
South of George Town
Tel: 949 7468 or 800 552 6281
A 35-room studio-apartment dive resort overlooking the ocean, with a pool, Jacuzzi, restaurant, bar, and unlimited shore diving both day and night. $$

Left: a traditional-style property on Cayman Brac

Comfort Suites
Seven Mile Beach
Tel: 945 7300
www.caymancomfort.com
These sensibly-priced but roomy suites contain full kitchens and high-speed data ports. There's a fitness center, scuba center, pool, laundry room, restaurant, and bar. $$

Driftwood Village
North Side
Tel: 947 9015
A very private complex of four, two-bedroom cottages with full kitchens and excellent fishing and diving from the shore. $$

Sunset House
George Town
Tel: 949 7111 or 800 854 4767
www.sunsethouse.com
Heralded as a hotel for scuba divers run by scuba divers, this is a down-to-earth place with comfortable rooms, a restaurant, bar, freshwater pool, hot tub, and a full-service dive operation that offers scuba certification classes, check-out dives, and advanced scuba training. $$

Sunshine Suites
Seven Mile Beach
Tel: 949 3000
www.sunshinesuites.com
One of the few low-cost properties on Seven Mile Beach, this has spacious rooms, fully-equipped kitchens, laundry facilities, cable TV, and a pool. It's not on the ocean, but guests have access to a private beach. $$

Adam's Guest House
George Town
Tel: 949 2512
A friendly little inn in a private house with six air-conditioned rooms with private baths and kitchens. Walking distance of downtown. $

Eldemire's Guest House
George Town
Tel: 949 5385
In a quiet neighborhood about 1 mile (1.6 km) south of George Town, walking distance of Smith Cove, this 13-room inn has kitchen access, laundry, and private baths. $

Seaview Hotel
George Town
Tel: 945 0558
On the south side of George Town, this 15-room hotel has a dive center, saltwater pool, gourmet dining room, and piano bar. $

Cayman Brac
Carib Sands
South Side West
Tel: 948 1121
www.caribsands.com
A modern, ocean-front complex with one- and two-bedroom apartments, a beautiful beach, water-sports, restaurant, and bar. $$$

Almond Beach Cottages
Spot Bay
Tel: 948 0667 or 800 972 9795
A small, luxurious three-unit property with spacious two-bedroom cottages, terraces and snorkeling just steps from the hotel. $$

Above: elegant accommodations on Cayman Brac, seen from the air

Brac Reef Beach Resort
South Side West
Tel: 948 1323 or 800 327 3835
www.bracreef.com
A casual, relaxed dive resort set in 5 acres (0.5 ha) with a wide, white beach. Restaurant, bar, tennis, dock, gym, Jacuzzi, pool, photo lab, and full-service dive center. $$

Divi Tirara Beach Resort
South Side West
Tel: 948 1553
A plush resort two-story; private beach, fresh-water pool, volleyball, tennis, and dive shop. $$

The Turtle Nest
Stake Bay
Tel: 948 1370
A small, fully-furnished private house; sleeps four. Tropical atmosphere; full-size kitchen and pool. $$

Walton's Mango Manor Guest House
Stake Bay
Tel: 948 0518
www.waltonsmangomanor.com
A small island-style getaway in a private home, with five rooms, private baths, laundry facilities, and breakfast included. $

Little Cayman
Conch Club Condominiums
Blossom Village
Tel: 948 1033 or 800 327 3835
Twelve plush, ocean-front two- and three-bedroom units; two pools, two docks, Jacuzzi, private beach, dive services. $$$

Pirates Point Resort
Preston Bay
Tel: 948 1010
Owned by award-winning chef, Gladys Howard, this delightful 10-room resort has a lively yet relaxed atmosphere, freshwater pool, full dive services, help-yourself-bar, and three gourmet meals a day. $$$

Little Cayman Beach Resort
Blossom Village
Tel: 948 1033 or 800 327 3835
www.littlecayman.com
Upscale dive resort with a full-service dive

and photo shop, restaurant, bar, gym, and games room. $$

McCoy's Diving and Fishing Lodge
Bloody Bay
Tel: 948 0026 or 800 626 0496
A rustic eight-room lodge with a quaint atmosphere, freshwater pool, bar, restaurant, fishing, and diving facilities. $$

Suzy's Cottage
Blossom Village
Tel: 945 4144
A small beach-front cottage within walking distance of restaurants. It sleeps six and has a full kitchen and laundry facilities. $$

HEALTH/HYGIENE

One of the more developed places in the Caribbean, the Cayman Islands pose no health threats to visitors other than sunburn, heat stroke, insect bites, and 'the bends' (the effects of decompression due to coming to the surface too quickly when scuba diving). Because of the ferocity of the sun, the use of sun-block lotion is strongly recommended at all times of the year. Mosquito repellent should be used when hiking in Cayman Brac and at Queen Elizabeth II Botanic Park in Grand Cayman.

To avoid heat stroke and dehydration, especially in summer, take shelter from the sun at midday, always wear a hat, and drink plenty of fresh water. Desalination plants provide clean tap water that is safe to drink, and bottled water is readily available on the islands. Public restrooms are available at restaurants, most visitor attractions, shopping centers, and banks.

Medical/Dental Services/Pharmacies

It is always advisable to take out private medical insurance before you leave home, to cover the costs of any emergency care. The government-run George Town Hospital (tel: 949 8600) has a 24-hour emergency room as well as a decompression chamber for scuba divers. Cayman Brac has the Faith Hospital (tel: 948 2243), and Little Cayman has a small clinic (tel: 948 1051). Dialing 911

anywhere in the islands will connect you to emergency medical assistance.

There is also a Medivac air ambulance service (tel: 949 0241) that can fly passengers rapidly to major hospitals in Miami. For health problems that are not serious or life-threatening, walk-in clinics are available in Grand Cayman. Health care services are excellent, and pharmacies are abundant.

The following numbers may be useful if you need medical care:
Professional Medical Centre, Grand Cayman, tel: 949 6066.
Cayman Medical and Surgical Center, tel: 949 8150.
Island Chiropractic Center, tel: 945 1988.
Island Medical Associates, tel: 946 3324.
Cayman Dental Services, tel: 945 4447.
Merren Dental Center, tel: 949 2554.
Edmar's Discount Drugs, tel: 949 9800.
Foster's Pharmacy, tel: 945 7759.
Health Care Pharmacy, tel: 949 0442.

CRIME/TROUBLE

With an almost non-existent crime rate, the Cayman Islands is one of the safest places in the Caribbean. It is still advisable not to leave valuables unattended in cars or on the beach. In case of emergency, tel: 911 (toll-free) for both the police and fire departments.

Consulates
Consular assistance is available in Grand Cayman for US citizens (tel: 945 1511) and UK citizens (tel: 949 7900).

COMMUNICATIONS AND MEDIA

Mail
The main post office is on Edward Street in George Town (tel: 949 2474), and a dozen others are scattered throughout the islands. Most are open Mon–Fri, 8:30am–5pm and Sat 8:30am–noon. Postage stamps are available at most hotels and gift shops.

Telephone/Internet
All the Cayman Islands have excellent telecommunication services, and supposedly the largest number of fax machines per capita, due to the banking industry. The area code for all three islands is 345. It is not necessary to dial this code when placing on-island or inter-island calls. Information can be reached by dialing 411.

Local calls are charged by the minute. Public pay phones are located in most commercial areas, and cell phones are available for rent as well.

For calls to the US, US Sprint (888 366 46630), MCI Direct (800 624 1000), and AT&T Direct (800 872 2881) are available. Locally-purchased phone cards are convenient, and can be bought at many grocery stores, gas stations, and gift shops.

To place a call to the US, dial 1 + area code + number. To place a call to the UK, dial 011 + 44 + area code + local number. Most major hotels offer high-speed Internet hook-up services for guests, or you can use the following Internet cafés:
Café del Sol, West Bay Road, Grand Cayman, tel: 946 2233.
Dickens Internet Café, Galleria Plaza, Grand Cayman, tel: 945 9195.
Shooters, Seven Mile Shops, Grand Cayman, tel: 946 3496.
McLaughlin's, Village Square, Little Cayman, tel: 948 1000.

Television
So abundant is cable and satellite television in the Cayman Islands that local people joke about the satellite dish being the national bird. Needless to say, cable television programs from both the US and the UK are available in most hotels. There are also three local television channels and four radio stations.

practical information

Above: the island crime rate is very low but the police remain vigilant

Newspapers

The Cayman Islands has one daily newspaper, the *Caymanian Compass*, which is sold in stores throughout the islands. Newspapers from the US and the UK can also be found at large hotels and book stores. Several of the larger chain hotels subscribe to the *New York Times* fax service which provides a condensed version of the day's news.

USEFUL INFORMATION

Visitors with disabilities

Most hotels and restaurants are wheelchair-accessible, as are transportation vans from the airport. For special assistance, Elite Limousine Service (tel: 949 5963) is available for transportation, and the Health Care Pharmacy (tel: 949 0442) is a useful, specialized store.

Children

Most major resorts offer baby-sitting services, activities for children, and special programs for teenagers. Child-friendly specialty spots include:
O2B Kidz Funzone, West Bay Road, Grand Cayman, tel: 946 5439.
Planet Arcadia, Grand Harbour Centre, Grand Cayman, tel: 947 4263.

Smyles Playtime Paradise Islander Complex, Grand Cayman, tel: 946 5800.

Gays/Lesbians

Unfortunately, the Cayman Islands is not a gay/lesbian-friendly destination. In the late 1990s, the government turned away a cruise ship full of gay passengers that had planned on docking in the port, and ever since it has been regarded as intolerant by gay and human rights groups in North America. This is not to say there are no gays or lesbians on the islands; they just intentionally keep a low profile.

SPORT

Although scuba diving and snorkeling are the sports of choice, golf, fishing, horseback riding, sailing, windsurfing, and kayaking are also popular. Most large hotels have their own pools and tennis courts.

Diving/Snorkeling
Grand Cayman:
Abanks Divers, tel: 945 1444.
Aquanauts Diving, tel: 945 1990.
Bob Soto's Diving, tel: 949 2871.
Dive Cayman, tel: 945 5770.
Divers Down, tel: 945 1611.
Don Foster's Dive, tel: 949 5679.
Ocean Frontiers, tel: 947 7500.
Treasure Island Divers, tel: 949 4456.
Cayman Brac and **Little Cayman**: Most resorts on the sister islands offer their own dive services.

Golf
Britannia Golf Club, Grand Cayman, tel: 949 8020.
Links at Safe Haven, Grand Cayman, tel: 949 5988.
Sunrise Family Golf Centre, Grand Cayman, tel: 947 4653.

Horseback riding
Honeysuckle Trails, Grand Cayman, tel: 947 7976.
Nicki's Beach Rides, Grand Cayman, tel: 945 5839.
Pampered Ponies, Grand Cayman, tel: 945 2262.

Above: you don't have to do your own fishing – the George Town Fish Market can supply all you need

practical information

Fishing
Cayman Islands Angling Club, Grand Cayman, tel: 945 3131.
Charter Boat Headquarters, Grand Cayman, tel: 945 4340.
Chip-Chip Fishing Charters, Grand Cayman, tel: 947 1093.
Island Girl Charters, Grand Cayman, tel: 947 3029.
Just Fishin', Grand Cayman, tel: 916 0113.

Sailing/Windsurfing/Kayaking
Barefoot Water-sports, Cayman Brac, tel: 948 1299.
Cayman Kayak Adventures, Grand Cayman, tel: 926 1234.
Cayman Windsurf, Grand Cayman, tel: 947 7492.
Red Baron Charters, Grand Cayman, tel: 945 4744.
Red Sail Water-sports, Grand Cayman, tel: 945 5965.
Sailboards Caribbean, Grand Cayman, tel: 949 1068.
Seasports, Grand Cayman, tel: 949 3965.

Parasailing
Parasailing Professionals, Grand Cayman, tel: 916 2953.

Bowling
Stingray Bowling Center and Arcade, Grand Cayman, tel: 945 4444.

USEFUL ADDRESSES

Tourist Offices
Cayman Islands Department of Tourism
The Pavilion, Cricket Square
George Town, Grand Cayman
Tel: 949 0623
www.caymanislands.ky or
www.divecayman.ky
United Kingdom
6 Arlington Street
London, SW1A 1RE
Tel: 44 (0) 207 491 7771.
USA
420 Lexington Avenue
New York, NY 10170
Tel: 800 346 3313.
Canada, tel: 416 485 1550.

Germany/Austria/Benelux, tel: 49 69 60 320 94.
France, tel: 33 1 53 424136.

Airlines
Cayman Airways, Grand Cayman, tel: 949 2311.
UK, tel: 44 (0) 207 491 7771.
US/Canada, tel: 800 422 9626.
Website: www.caymanairways.com
Island Air, Grand Cayman, tel: 949 0241.
Website: www.islandaircayman.com
Air Jamaica, tel: 949 2300.
American Airlines, tel: 949 0666.
British Airways, tel: 949 2311.
Delta Air Lines, tel: 945 8431.
US Air, tel: 949 7488.

Booking Agents
The following agents offer travel assistance to US and Canadian tourists:
Cayman Islands Reservation Service, tel: 800 235 5888. International Travel and Resorts, tel: 800 223 9815.

FURTHER READING

Brief History of the Caribbean, Jan Rogozinski, Facts on File, 1992.
A Continent of Islands, Mark Kurlansky, Addison-Wesley, 1992.
Birds of the Cayman Islands, Patricia Bradley, World Publications, 1985.
Caribbean, James A Michener, Random House, 1989.
Cayman Islands Dive Guide, Stephen Frink, Abbeville Press, 1999.
Cayman Islands, The Martha K Smith, Cuchipanda Inc, 1995.
Cookin' in Little Cayman, Gladys Howard, Little Cayman National Trust, 1996.
Dive Sites of the Cayman Islands, Lawson Wood, Passport Books, 1998.
Flora of the Cayman Islands, G R Procter, Royal Botanic Gardens, 1984.
Guide to the Reef Fish of the Cayman Islands, Rod MacPherson, Nature World Press, 1995.
Maritime Heritage of the Cayman Islands, Roger C Smith, Univ. Press of Florida, 2001.
Second Wind, Dick Francis, Random House, 2000.

INSIGHT
Pocket Guides

Insight Pocket Guides pioneered a new approach to guidebooks, introducing the concept of the authors as "local hosts" who would provide readers with personal recommendations, just as they would give honest advice to a friend who came to stay. They also included a full-size pull-out map. Now, to cope with the needs of the 21st century, new editions in this growing series are being given a new look to make them more practical to use, and restaurant and hotel listings have been greatly expanded.

credits

ACKNOWLEDGEMENTS

10, 11, 12 **AKG London**
16 **Cayman Islands National Archive**
2/3, 20, 51B, 52, 53T, 54, 58, 59, 65T **Wolfgang Tins/Terraqua**

Front cover **Pictures Colour Library**
Back cover **Phil Wood**

Cartography **Berndtson & Berndtson**

© APA Publications GmbH & Co. Verlag KG Singapore Branch, Singapore

INDEX